Editor:
City of Kaiserslautern
Advertisement agencies ANTARES,
Höhn Communication, vis@vis

© Copyright for texts and photos:
City Administration Kaiserslautern,
Willy-Brandt-Platz 1, 67657 Kaiserslautern, Germany
www.kaiserslautern.de

Front page design:
Höhn Communication

Front page photo:
Jörg Heieck, view - Reiner Voß

Overall concept:
Advertisement agencies ANTARES,
Höhn Communication, vis@vis

Text:
Dirk A. Leibfried

Translation:
Sonnhild Namingha

Design:
ANTARES Werbeagentur
Pages 75-129

Höhn Communication
Pages 3-74; 130-192

Printed by:
Kerker Druck, Kaiserslautern, Germany

Reprinting of this book, either in whole or in parts, as well as the use of any texts or photos contained therein is illegal and prohibited. The editor reserves the copyright and all further rights. Translation, storage, reproduction, and dissemination, including transfer to electronic media such as video text, Internet, etc., are prohibited without express permission and thus punishable by law.

ISBN 3-9806804-4-4

Photo credits:

view - die agentur, Kaiserslautern

Corinna Voß: Page 56, 58, 61, 70, 91, 102, 103, 104, 105, 113, 115, 128, 130, 131, 132, 136, 137, 142

Darius Simka: Page 5, 6, 12, 55, 57, 67, 78, 80, 94, 98, 100, 101, 103, 104, 106, 108, 110, 113, 116, 122, 128, 132, 133, 134, 135, 136, 138, 139, 140, 141, 146, 152, 153, 171, 176, 180, 182, 185

Isabell Girard de Soucanton: Page 18, 19, 191

Julia Heinrich: Page 10, 11, 22, 28, 32, 54, 56, 59, 62, 63, 73, 78, 81, 86, 89, 94, 96, 100, 102, 104, 105, 109, 110, 111, 114, 117, 122, 145, 147, 148, 155, 169, 178

Michael Schäfer: Page 3, 11, 12, 13, 17, 38, 40, 41, 44, 45, 47, 49, 57, 58, 83, 85, 87, 89, 90, 91, 92, 93, 95, 96, 97, 101, 110, 111, 117, 127, 131, 144, 153, 155, 157, 168, 172, 173, 177, 185

Reiner Voß: Page 9, 14, 15, 16, 20, 21, 23, 28, 30, 32, 33, 34, 35, 36, 37, 42, 43, 51, 52, 53, 55, 59, 63, 69, 76, 77, 79, 80, 82, 83, 86, 87, 89, 91, 92, 95, 97, 98, 99, 101, 102, 103, 106, 107, 108, 112, 116, 120, 121, 124, 125, 126, 127, 129, 131, 132, 145, 146, 151, 152, 153, 154, 159, 162, 168, 175, 176, 179, 180, 181, 182, 185, 186, 188, 190, 192, 193

Sabine Blatt: Page 61, 72, 109, 110, 113

City Administration Kaiserslautern

Hanni Beck: Page 13, 17, 24, 28, 29, 31, 39, 41, 55, 60, 61, 74, 84, 85, 88, 89, 90, 93, 95, 99, 105, 116, 122, 123, 144, 145, 146, 149, 151, 156, 158, 159, 160, 161, 162, 163, 164, 165, 167, 178, 179, 183, 188, 189

Manfred Schuck: Page 43, 45, 55, 56, 67, 70, 80, 82, 86, 87, 88, 110, 112, 151

Marc Breitinger: Page 114

Pascal Przybyla: Page 29

Jörg Heieck, Kaiserslautern
Page 7, 8, 39, 45, 46, 47, 63, 65, 68, 73, 97, 120, 141, 142, 143, 145, 147, 150, 151, 170, 171, 175, 176, 183

ANTARES, Kaiserslautern
Page 24, 25, 162, 185

Dirk A. Leibfried, Kaiserslautern
Page 23, 27

Höhn Communication, Kaiserslautern
Page 17, 23, 26, 27, 28, 47, 157, 164, 165

Martin Barth, Kaiserslautern
Page 44, 48, 50, 56, 60, 62, 66, 68, 70, 72, 118, 119, 174, 178, 182, 183, 185

Others

Bauer/Quitsch, Kaiserslautern
Page 56, 57, 58, 64

dpa Picture-Alliance, Frankfurt
Page 16, 26

JJ-Medien, Saarbrücken
Page 126

Trellenkamp, Kaiserslautern
Page 119

Miscellaneous
Page 40, 42, 51, 55, 69, 70, 71, 72, 179, 180, 184, 185

Campaigns:

ANTARES Werbeagentur, Kaiserslautern
Congeniality Campaign, pages 24-25

Höhn Communication, Kaiserslautern
Site Campaign, pages 26-27,
World Cup Gallery, pages 164-165

Table of Contents

- Preface: Lord Mayor Bernhard J. Deubig .... pp. 8 - 9
- Essay .... pp. 10 - 13
- Prelude: Application and campaigns .... pp. 14 - 29
- A stadium achieves global reputation .... pp. 30 - 37
- Five matches for eternity .... pp. 38 - 49
- The big party .... pp. 50 - 69
- Encounters .... pp. 70 - 74
- Diary .... pp. 75 - 129

- Emotions .... pp. 130 - 141
  - A time to make friends .... pp. 142 - 149
- The whole city is World Cup .... pp. 150 - 155
  - All "dressed up" .... pp. 156 - 167
- Discoveries .... pp. 168 - 177
  - Many hard-working helpers .... pp. 178 - 185
- Statistics .... pp. 186 - 187
  - Words of thanks and tribute .... pp. 188 - 189
- Epilogue: World Cup Coordinator Erwin Saile .... pp. 190 - 191

QUOTE ...

"I FIND it great that I am no longer the only one with a flag on my car."

Horst Köhler,
German President

Preface
Lord Mayor Bernhard J. Deubig

"Immense image gain is invaluable"

The slogan "Smallest city, biggest fun", which Kaiserslautern as the smallest of the World Cup Host Cities had communicated worldwide long before the matches started, admittedly was imbued with very much hope, even if the confidence of the city, in which soccer can be said to incorporate and symbolize "body and soul", which had won several German championships, and from whose Betzenberg half of the team of the "Heroes of Bern" in 1954 hailed, was, by all means, justified. But now, after the matches, it is certain: Kaiserslautern managed to demonstrate to the world how the modern Kaiserslautern really is: an international city, where 130 different nationalities live together peacefully, cosmopolitan, multi-cultural, charmingly hospitable, and totally likeable. Weeks after the World Cup, letters, faxes, and emails continue to arrive every day, saying nothing but: It was nice to stay with you – we will come back! The immense image gain represents an almost priceless value.

This indescribable feedback from all parts of the world – Japan, Australia, South America and the USA as well as Arabia and the countries of the EU – not only affects the emotional sensors, but also shows real effects: Examples include the decision of a Japanese global player to choose Kaiserslautern as the site for its first European development center, and the intensification of the traditionally very good relations to the North American business world. Not to mention the new, very positive encounters with Australians, who literally experienced the modern Kaiserslautern as a successful information and communications high-tech site ("From Goal Producer to Think Tank" was one of the city's World Cup slogans) with their hearts and minds.

One of the most important events of the World Cup, however, is the change in the minds of the citizens of Kaiserslautern. The number of "avowed converts" is sensationally large: "I had reservations, but I must admit – this was good!" This encourages us to face the future with confidence.

In retrospect, we must not forget to mention, of course, that the preliminary phase of the matches brought approximately 150 million euros worth of investments into the infrastructure and the development of the city. These projects, which served as a great incentive to the local economy, ensure long-term benefits for the city, benefits which otherwise would not have been realized in this way, at this speed, or not at all.

"KL" is proud that – without exception – this was a "precision landing". I would like to express my thanks, my appreciation, and my great enthusiasm for those responsible because of their official duties, for the many voluntary helpers, and for the citizens of our city, who all came together to form a wonderful team, by saying

"THANK YOU SOCCER,
       THANK YOU 2006 FIFA WORLD CUP,
  THANK YOU KAISERSLAUTERN!"

Bernhard J. Deubig
Lord Mayor of the
FIFA World Cup Host City Kaiserslautern

A toast to success in heaven:
Gracious dancers, plastic kangaroos, and removable tattoos

Match over. Where just a short time ago flag-waving fans were loudly dreaming of the "finals", where Australians walked through the alleys hand in hand with plastic kangaroos dreaming of "Mathilda", where Italians dug out the 1990s World Cup song by Gianna Nanini because Grönemeyer apparently was too hard to pronounce, where colorful costumes from the Caribbean nation of Trinidad and Tobago made people long for faraway places and the steel drums turned stiff oak trees into gracious dancers – normality has returned some time ago. Quietness. As though someone showed up overnight to stop the party. And pulled the plug. Just like that. Without prior warning. In other words: The city has been left to itself again.

Some say it was only a game. And yet, it was so much more: The World Cup has changed the city. And its people. The whole country exemplified it, Kaiserslautern as the smallest of the twelve World Cup host cities perfected it. And showed how we really are: cosmopolitan, multi-cultural, charming. So much so that it almost scared the guests: "This is how friendly the Germans are?" From the windows, flags of the teams playing in Kaiserslautern were flying; even in the normally scrupulously arranged flower boxes, flags from all countries could be seen: Stars and Stripes side by side with local geraniums.

It is not only the guests who make a great event into something that will later be called a mega-event. But they contribute a lot to it. Very few people would have imagined that people would be able to turn what used to be a tranquil downtown area into a surfers' beach. Inflatable plastic kangaroos not only served as good luck charms, but also as an excuse for ordering two beers at a time without having a bad conscience: "This one's for the kangaroo!" Often, the only thing that helped was to cool off. When Rick Springfield and AC/DC were played, the alarm level was red. The Australians rocked themselves into the hearts of the people, who secretly already decided to have a city partnership on the fifth continent.

"If you don't live now, you will not experience anything. If you don't move now, you will wait forever." The official World Cup song sounded from the loudspeakers without interruption. "Time for things to move." And in Kaiserslautern, the wheels may have turned even a little faster than in other places. There was a perfect liaison between effective organization and Mediterranean serenity. A party lasting 31 days took hold of the whole country, and we were farther away from the horror scenarios envisioned before the World Cup than Zinédine Zidane was from getting the fair-play trophy. Instead of tanks in front of the stadiums, police officers posed as photo subjects for foreign guests. In Kaiserslautern, the crime rate dropped during the World Cup...

COSMOPOLITAN, MULTI-CULTURAL, AND CHARMING: **This is how Kaiserslautern presented itself during the World Cup.**

A toast
to success in heaven: Gracious dancers, plastic kangaroos, and removable tattoos

Sometimes, the scenes appeared to be unreal: In street-side cafes, at the numerous stands, at the lake, on the streets, on terraces and balconies one could see people enjoying the moment. Each one in his or her own way. Over and over again. For four weeks. "You feel, you dream, you feel, you think you are flying." Even nature played along, combining sun, air, and water into a totally new, strange fluid. Something that Germans may have only known in this way from vacations in Italy. Germany definitely slid south on the temperament map and said good-bye to the image of the unfriendly, rude German for good. Yes, Germans can celebrate! Exuberantly, peacefully, and in unimagined dimensions. With fake Iroquois haircuts in black-red-gold and removable tattoos on the cheeks. Never before has a World Cup motto, which was initially smiled at condescendingly, been realized in such a way. The world was really a guest among friends. It really was A Time to Make Friends.

Just like the tourist visiting Liverpool expects to see a mop-top at each corner, or hears one Beatles song after the other in reality or in his imagination, the fascination of the "Miracle of Bern" could once again be felt close up during the weeks of the World Cup. Over-dimensional pictures of the 1954 World Champions characterized the cityscape, creating a bridge between then and now. Between the "eleven-friends-you-must-be" philosophy and the millions of euros that Francesco Totti earns today. The contradiction merged into the party – and into memories. Without any bitterness about how things have developed. The world has continued to revolve. Which does not mean that we cannot look at old pictures and reminisce every once in a while.

BIZARRE: **Fans from the United States and the Italian response to Elvis.**

It is such a pity that Fritz Walter did not live to experience the World Cup, which he had brought to Kaiserslautern, live in his stadium. But call it a quirk of fate that the later World Cup champion "Italia" paraded twice in the World Cup arena in Kaiserslautern, and that thus his wife's first name was omnipresent, phonetically at least. In heaven, they also have Prosecco to drink to this success. They certainly do.

Memories last the longest, they say. And this World Cup will likely stay in the memories of the people in Kaiserslautern, in the Palatinate, forever. Of course, Germany, and the Germans, have done a lot for their image in the world. This helps. In diplomatic circles. Sooner or later also in tourism. But the World Cup host city Kaiserslautern has also learned its own positive lessons: We can do it! The smallest metropolis shook off the image of provinciality within a few weeks, in order to play along in the concert of the big ones. And wherever it was necessary, it managed to again pull a trump by being provincial, so that it could stand out from the others. This is how we are! Loveable hosts, cosmopolitan, helpful. Those who still have doubts about this have missed the World Cup.

And this was something that could be observed not only in Kaiserslautern, but in the entire country: The countless flags, banners, pennants, scarves and hats, the many flashy creations of "partyotism" mainly expressed something that can be seen mostly among the younger generation: a liberation from the perpetual German self-distrust, from the notorious suspicion against oneself, from saying a priori "Yes, but – may we really do this ...?"

We may! Never before have so many people been in Kaiserslautern within such a short time. There were encounters, discoveries, emotions. People from very different cultural areas became friends. They understood each other, without necessarily speaking the other one's language. Soccer can do that. A World Cup especially. And therefore, the decision to host this World Cup in Kaiserslautern was the right decision. A far-reaching one. A historical one. "There is no choice and no second time", sings Grönemeyer.

This is something that we could have known earlier, but sometimes it is necessary to experience an event on one's own in order to arrive at such an insight. This wonderful event was the 2006 FIFA World Cup in Kaiserslautern.

VOICES ...

"NONE OF our other World Cup host cities has this! The city of Kaiserslautern counted close to 150,000 visitors on Saturday for the match Italy against USA – one and a half times as many people as the population of this Palatine city! ... 'The atmosphere here is almost better than inside the stadium', said a surprised visitor from Frankfurt. 'World class', was the enthusiastic comment of another one from Bad Hersfeld: 'An absolutely cool World Cup venue!'"

BILD, Germany

Prelude
Application and campaigns

On 15 April 2002 at 3.05 p.m. it was a fact: Kaiserslautern will be a host city for the 2006 FIFA World Cup. Thousands of people celebrated in the city when the decision was broadcast from Alte Oper in Frankfurt on the public viewing screen. The approval was preceded by an application marathon, which was briefly interrupted when funding for the stadium's extension and modernization was at risk due to the financial calamity of the 1. FC Kaiserslautern.

2000
2001
2002
2003
2004
2005
2006

OFFICIAL: Kaiserslautern will host the 2006 FIFA World Cup. The Lord Mayors of the twelve host cities (below), among them Bernhard J. Deubig (top), are looking forward to a great soccer event.

KL
KAISERSLAUTERN

2000
2001
2002
2003
2004
2005
2006

On 13 October 2000, the 1. FC Kaiserslautern, the state of Rheinland-Pfalz, and the city of Kaiserslautern jointly submitted an application to become a Host City, after Germany had received approval to host the 2006 FIFA World Cup. Fritz Walter took over the role of World Cup Ambassador. His contributions were a major reason why World Cup matches would take place in the stadium that bears his name.

HEROIC: Franz Beckenbauer (right) knows how important the "Heroes of Bern" are (from the left, Ottmar Walter, Horst Eckel, and Fritz Walter).

"Five World Champions and Kaiserslautern: 2006 FIFA World Cup – We are ready.": In November 2001, Fritz and Ottmar Walter, Horst Eckel, Andreas Brehme, and Youri Djorkaeff agreed to having their joint picture used for an application poster. An image film about the city was produced to further impress the Organizing Committee. On 5 December 2001, the official application documents were submitted in Frankfurt. In reality, the so-called "specification document" turned out to be a collection of binders with several hundred pages.

50 years after the "Miracle of Bern", the final match of Germany versus Hungary was "replayed" in Kaiserslautern. An exhibit in the "Kammgarn" Cultural Center provided a reminder to the heroes of the past. And almost unnoticed at first, the World Cup fever in Kaiserslautern continued to rise.

PRELUDE: *Interior Minister Walter Zuber, Horst Eckel, Fritz Walter, Minister President Kurt Beck, Ottmar Walter, and Lord Mayor Bernhard J. Deubig submitting the application of Kaiserslautern as a World Cup Host City.*

OFFICIAL: *The two heads of state of Hungary and Germany signed the city's Golden Book 50 years after the "Miracle of Bern". From the left: Lord Mayor Bernhard J. Deubig, Ferenc Mádel, and Johannes Rau.*

Feiern, genießen und erinnern vor dem
Fußball-Länderspiel Deutschland - Ungarn

Aus, aus, aus, aus!
Das Spiel beginnt

6. Juni 2004
10:30-19 Uhr
Willy-Brandt-Platz

- Ungarisches Militärorchester
  Kalocsa Helyörsèg Fùvòszenkara
- Romeo Franz Ensemble – Hot Swing and more
- Duo Piroschka – ungarisches Geiger-Duo
- Heinz Kober – „Live"-Moderation WM-Finale 1954
- Timo Menge – „Ein Stück Kaiserslautern"
- 50 Jahre „Wunder von Bern"
  Präsentation des Festwagens
- Ungarische Leckereien von der Wartenberger Mühle

Eine Veranstaltung des WM-Büros Kaiserslautern

KL STADT KAISERSLAUTERN

COMMITTED: *Took over the role of World Cup Ambassador after the death of Fritz Walter: Horst Eckel.*

2000
2001
2002
2003
2004
2005
2006

Soccer Fever 1 Prelude: Application and campaigns   17

2000
2001
2002
2003
2004
2005
2006

Prelude
Application and campaigns

"Stars around the Ball" was the name of a series of events. The so-called "Preparation Games for the 2006 FIFA World Cup", which took place in cooperation with the World Cup Office of Kaiserslautern and the Kammgarn Cultural Center, cast a spell on Stiftsplatz. Highlights certainly included the performances of world star Peter Gabriel and singer Helmut Lotti. In the spring of 2006, more "pre-games" took place at the Kammgarn: The four first-round encounters at Fritz-Walter-Stadion were performed on stage by various artists, featuring Australian comedy, exotic performances, and world star Melanie.

Soccer Fever Prelude: Application and campaigns

2000
2001
2002
2003
2004
2005
2006

The fact that Kaiserslautern now really was a World Cup Host City became visible to everyone between 17 May and 19 June 2005. The World Cup Globe, a 20-meter high globe of the world designed like a ball, was set up on Alter Theaterplatz. A grandiose spectacle about one year before the World Cup.

Numerous attractions inside the globe, including interactive games, virtual installations, and panorama projections, as well as many events attracted almost 40,000 visitors within one month.

VOICES ...

"SCEPTICS abounded when the Palatine metropolis Kaiserslautern was accepted into the illustrious circle of the 2006 FIFA World Cup Host Cities. 'City too small, roads too narrow, stadium too far up', were comments that could be heard from critics over and over. The smallest World Cup host city has now gotten over and done with its five matches with bravura and excellence. Looking back, the 'experiment Kaiserslautern' may be called a success."

Allgemeine Zeitung, Germany

■ ■ ■

Prelude
Application and campaigns

2000
2001
2002
2003
2004
2005
2006

GREAT HONOR FOR KAISERSLAUTERN: Exactly 100 days before the start of the 2006 FIFA World Cup, the official admission ticket was presented. And this was done – very good for publicity – at the city hall in Kaiserslautern. OC Vice-Chairman Wolfgang Niersbach and World Cup mascot Goleo VI attracted about 150 representatives of the media to the ticket presentation. A smile for the photographers: Erwin Saile, René C. Jäggi, and Berhard J. Deubig.

Things got really "serious" for the first time on 9 December 2005, when the drawing for the groups took place in Leipzig. From one moment to the next, the World Cup fever among the organizers rose – as did their anticipation towards a great soccer festival. The match schedule with its cryptic abbreviations now finally got a face – and names. The city with Lord Mayor Bernhard J. Deubig and World Cup Coordinator Erwin Saile, the Organizing Committee outpost with its chairman Hans-Peter Schössler and manager René C. Jäggi, as well as the state with Minister President Kurt Beck and World Cup representative Dr. Franz-Josef Kemper demonstrated unity: Together we will do it!

BUSINESS CARD: The Media Box of the World Cup Host City Kaiserslautern received a lot of praise during the drawing in Leipzig, where journalists from all over the world could get information about the city (left).

2000
2001
2002
2003
2004
2005
2006

Prelude
Application and campaigns

In the meantime, a new media star was born: Elsa, the 69-year-old World Cup grandma. She appealed to the citizens of Kaiserslautern to be good and friendly hosts: "When the world arrives, I will go there!" Whether the credit was only Elsa's that this statement was fulfilled in such an impressive way?

Elsa cooked, Elsa fixed her garden, Elsa learned foreign languages, Elsa put on make-up for the great event: The World Cup grandma showed herself as the perfect hostess on posters and advertisements. And carried this message into the city and the region.

The twelve host cities of the 2006 FIFA World Cup presented themselves to the world with individual motives. Kaiserslautern advertised itself with the motive "IT", which was selected as the official host city poster by almost 3,000 citizens.

The poster was used by both FIFA and the city and was meant to represent the host city globally as an attractive and future-oriented business site. There is hardly any other city with such a high concentration of IT technology and research as Kaiserslautern. The poster was designed by Edgar Gerhards (ANTARES Werbeagentur).

The poster shows a computer circuit board, which, when viewed from a distance, represents the stadium. But there is also a human aspect, of course. The soldering points represent fans and players, who are connected among each other and with the city via conductors. The ball dynamically jumps at the viewer – and back into the game.

VOTED ON: *The official poster of the World Cup Host City Kaiserslautern.*

2000
2001
2002
2003
2004
2005
2006

Marketing activities before the World Cup concentrated not only on the Elsa campaign, but also on the much-noted site campaign. Kaiserslautern used catchy slogans to advertise itself as an IT site in manager magazines, at airports, and in the government quarter in Berlin: "From Goal Producer to Think Tank". Minister President Kurt Beck and Lord Mayor Bernhard J. Deubig jointly presented the campaign in Berlin.

The city also wanted to use the 2006 FIFA World Cup to position itself as an IT site of the future. The World Cup Host City used its location off the beaten path to catch the interest of the so-called decision-makers in a charming and coquettish way: "If you find us, you'll like us" was the leitmotiv of the site campaign.

The future belongs to information and communications technology; some people are already talking about Germany's "Silicon Woods". Two Fraunhofer institutes, the new Max Planck institute, the German Institute for Artificial Intelligence (DFKI), the University of Kaiserslautern, and the University of Applied Sciences represent young sciences and the intensive collaboration of business with mostly young and innovative companies. In the areas of industrial mathematics, software engineering, computer science, nanotechnology, and laser technology as well as artificial intelligence, the city boasts excellent competencies.

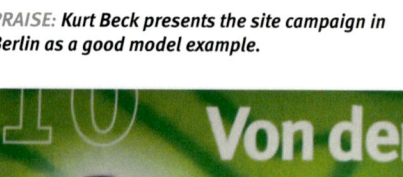
PRAISE: *Kurt Beck presents the site campaign in Berlin as a good model example.*

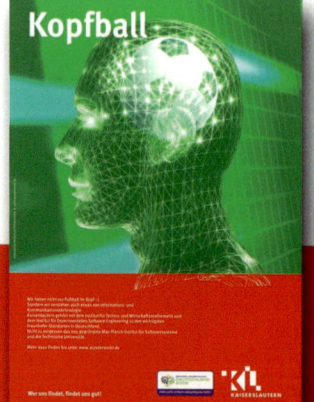

Making national and international decision makers and managers aware of this was the intention of the site campaign. In economic magazines such as Financial Times Deutschland, Handelsblatt, Wirtschaftswoche, or Manager-Magazin, but also in airport business lounges, attention was called to Kaiserslautern.

The topic of technology was combined with the Palatine way of life, while at the same time making the connection to soccer. Provocative headlines and unusual motives were used to create interest.

Information technology even made its way into the reality of the World Cup: In collaboration with the German Center for Artificial Intelligence (DFKI), the City-Guide-Mobile, a navigation system for pedestrians, was developed.

CATCHY: *The motives of the IT campaign in front of the Rheinland-Pfalz representative office in Berlin. From the left: Erwin Saile, Hans Höhn, and Bernhard J. Deubig.*

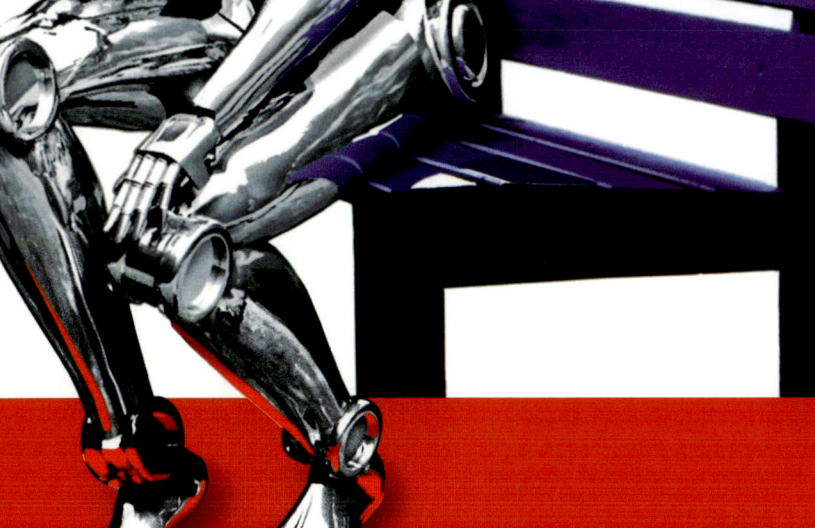

2000
2001
2002
2003
2004
2005
2006

Prelude
Application and campaigns

MOMENTS ...

EVEN PRIOR TO the World Cup, numerous companies, associations, and institutions prepared for the mega-event, including a group of about 50 Japanese hostesses and travel guides. In addition to visiting the Fritz-Walter-Stadion, these ladies also asked the Kaiserslautern World Cup Office for an introduction to the rules of soccer. The organizers were happy to accommodate this rather unusual request: A member of the World Cup Office staff is a hobby referee and introduced the ladies to the secrets of the offside rule and the four-man backfield defense.

■ ■ ■

Soccer and art? Soccer is art! And soccer can be represented artfully. Be it as a musical ("Abydos") or as a music show ("WM-Kult-Tour"). At the Pfalztheater, the impressive Lego model of Fritz-Walter-Stadion could be seen in addition to the robot dogs, at Theodor Zink Museum, visitors could experience the history of sports clothing close up. Under the motto "Fascination Soccer", a theme show at Pfalzgalerie dealt with the artistic perspective of the phenomenon soccer. Examples of how the game is reflected in visual arts and which effect it has on avant-gardists were shown. A World Cup studio in the exhibit was artfully designed as a studio setting, and sound documents and a video archive complemented the exhibit.

2000
2001
2002
2003
2004
2005
2006

KOINOBORI: 14 days before the World Cup, a 100-meter long fish made from colorful material, a so-called "Koinobori", rose into the sky above Kaiserslautern. It was a bow to the guests from Japan and the partner city of Bunkyo-ku.

A stadium achieves global reputation

A stadium achieves global reputation

On Betzenberg mountain, where Kaiserslautern's altitude is exactly 286.5 meters above sea level, soccer history has been written for decades. The arena has always been considered one of the nicest soccer stadiums in Germany. Passion, emotion, and enthusiasm are closely connected with this stadium. But the highlight for Fritz-Walter-Stadion have undoubtedly been the five World Cup matches.

A stadium achieves
global reputation

Before the 2006 FIFA World Cup, about 15 years of continuous development of the stadium were brought to an end with the upgrading of the Westside stands. 46,000 roofed seats were available during the World Cup; a media and a lounge tower complemented the modernization.

VOICES ...

"THE SOCCER STADIUM in Kaiserslautern thrones above the roofs of the city like a cathedral ... In order to support their team, the Socceroos, during the matches, many invested their annual vacation time. The costs for the expensive trip amount to 7,000 and 15,000 euros per person ... For the fans, this victory was worth crossing an entire planet, emptying their bank accounts, and sacrificing their entire annual leave."

Le Monde, France

Soccer Fever A stadium achieves global reputation

A stadium
achieves global reputation

SPECTACULAR: *In a very sophisticated technical procedure, the roof of the Southside stands was lifted 4.5 meters (15 feet) in September 2005. The lifting process was controlled by hydraulics. The goal was to connect the roofs of the Westside, Southside, and Eastside stands.*

In June 2003, the Fritz-Walter-Stadion as well as the training center for young players, the sports park "Rote Teufel (Red Devils)" were sold to a newly founded special purpose company, the municipal Fritz-Walter-Stadion Kaiserslautern GmbH. After completion of the Eastside stands (investments: 18.2 million euros), the capacity in this area increased from 9,365 to 14,959 seats. In November 2004, modernization of the rest began: The Southside stands were also expanded (1,302 more seats) as were the Westside stands (an additional 9,324 seats). Another 53 million euros had to be invested to make the stadium conform to World Cup standards.

Shortly before the World Cup, workers began to install the largest "solar power plant" in any soccer stadium on the roof of the Westside stands. On the roofs of three of the four stands, a photovoltaic system is expected to achieve a solar power output of up to 800 KWp on an area of approx. 6,000 square meters (1.5 acres) – which is the size of a soccer field. This equals the energy demand of about 200 single-family homes.

VOICES ...

"INTERESTED in a little quiz? What do you associate with Kaiserslautern? Forest? Correct. American soldiers? Correct. Soccer? Also correct. But actually, now it is almost only soccer which stands for this city in such a prominent and popular way. Hardly any German club provides so much identity for a region as the 1. FC Kaiserslautern. The citizens have built its stadium on top of Betzenberg mountain, reminiscent of a fortress that protects the city and into which its citizens may escape to take refuge."

Spiegel online, Germany

Soccer Fever | **37** A stadium achieves global reputation

KAISERSLAUTERN

Five matches for eternity

One may argue about the quality of the 64 World Cup matches played. However, there was certainly no revolution in world soccer with regard to tactics and playing system – and the cultivated offensive play of the German team almost remained an exception. The five encounters at Fritz-Walter-Stadion were a reflection of the entire World Cup: Strong defensive lines, restricted forward action, contested referee decisions, and a whole lot of yellow and red cards. Still: Together with Hamburg, Kaiserslautern is the only city in which the later world champion Italy played twice.

The atmosphere in the stadium could not be compared to that of a "regular" Bundesliga match. Exuberant, joyful. And noisy. This is how the fans of the respective teams presented themselves, as did the "neutral" visitors. And even hardcore fans felt the fascination exuded by such a World Cup when the national anthems were played. Goosebump feeling. And a few suppressed tears.

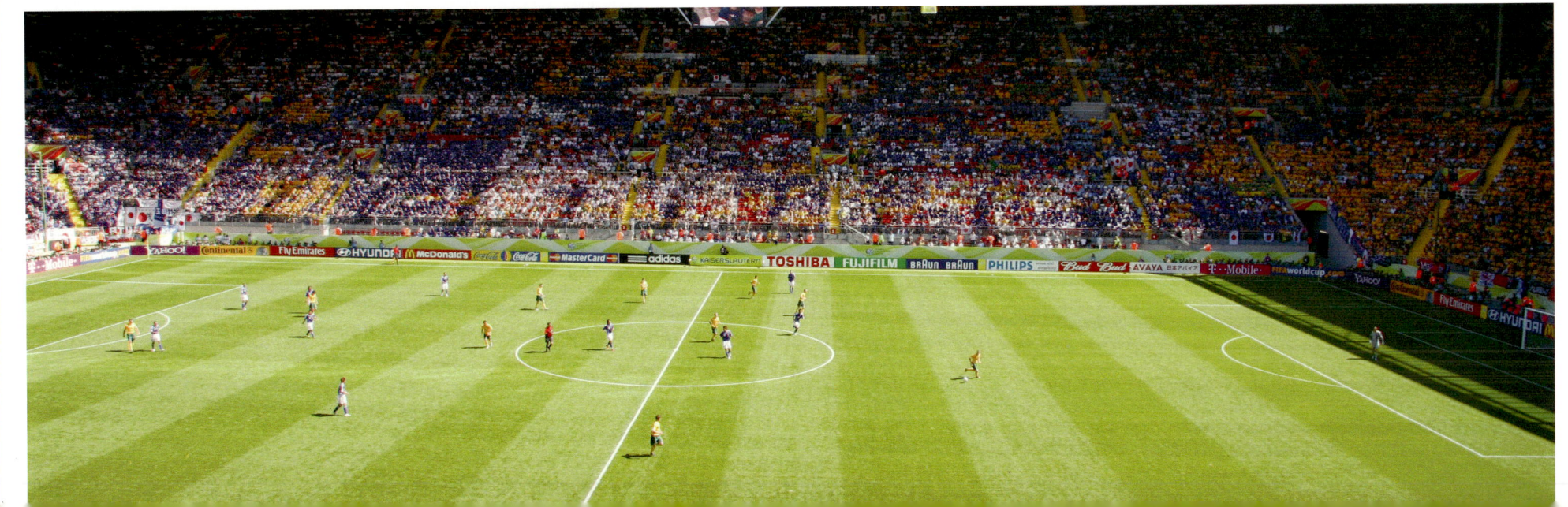

Soccer Fever Five matches for eternity

40

Monday, 12 June 2006

Australia – Japan 3:1

With a 3:1 victory over Japan, the Australians shot themselves into the tournament on 12 June – and into the hearts of the people of Kaiserslautern. At least as strong as his "Socceroos" on the field was their coach Guus Hiddink: "If you don't have a plan, you got to have luck. But my plan was to force luck." His replacement players Cahill and Aloisi turned a 0:1 deficit into a 3:1 victory during the last minutes of the match.

Gillette
TOSHIBA
FUJIFILM
DURACELL
PHILIPS
adidas
YAHOO!
Fly Emirates
HYUNDAI
MasterCard

TORRE
2
16

Saturday, 17 June 2006
Italy – USA 1:1

Five days later, Italy and the USA played 1:1. However, this match will not make it into the history books because of this rather commonplace result, but because of a total of three players being sent off from the match: First, Italy's Daniele de Rossi saw the red card, before the two U.S. Americans Pablo Mastroeni (red) and Eddie Pope (yellow-red) were also sent to the showers prematurely.

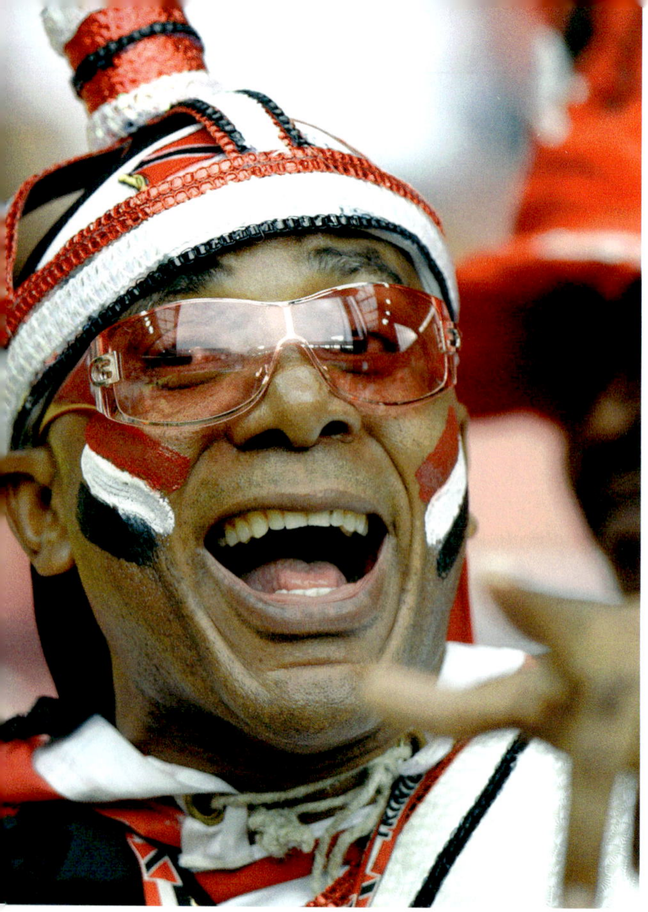

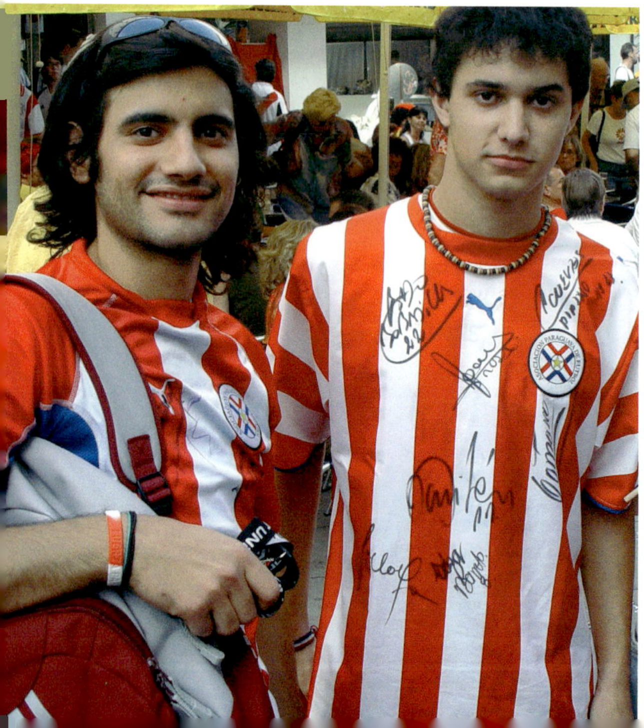

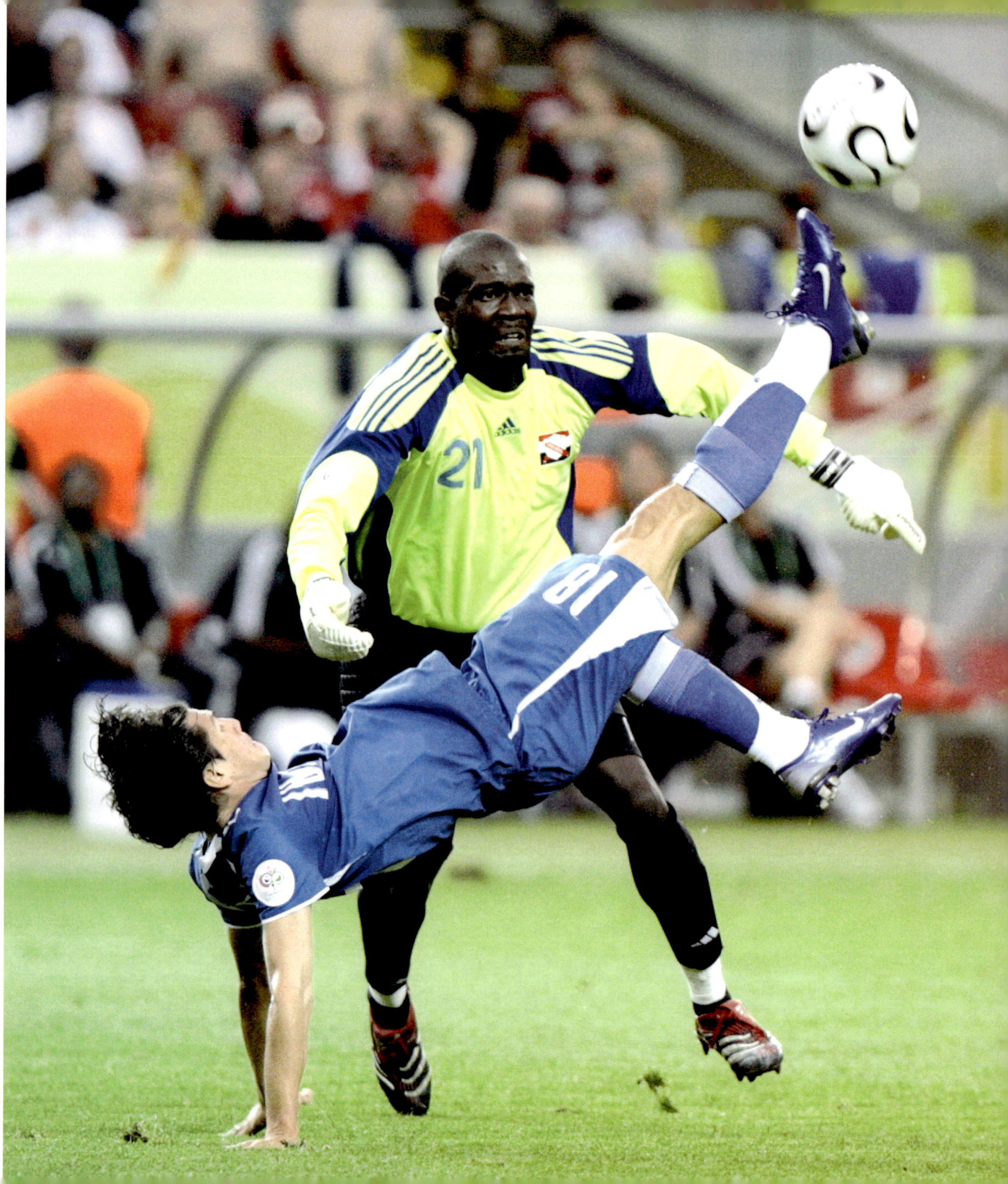
21

Paraguay – Trinidad & Tobago

Tuesday, 20 June 2006

Paraguay – Trinidad & Tobago 2:0

On 20 June, Paraguay celebrated a conciliatory end to the World Cup with a 2:0 victory over Trinidad and Tobago, despite the fact that before the match, the players from the Caribbean even had theoretical chances to make it into the next round. The marketing experts from Trinidad and Tobago had thought of something special for this match: In front of the stadium gates, they gave away T-shirts in the national colors – thus creating the impression that almost all the visitors in the stadium were real fans. And to some extent, this was true, of course...

VOICES...

"I WILL NEVER FORGET Kaiserslautern ... Trinidad and Tobago's proudest moment may have been the 0:0 against Sweden. But the most impressive thing for our tiny country was the fact that the hosts in Kaiserslautern gave us their hearts. The 'Soca Warriors' came to Germany hoping to be recognized as a people and as a soccer team. We think that we have achieved this – thanks to wonderful hosts ... The World Cup in Germany with its fan fests and spontaneous parties was perfect for us. Germany called the tournament 'a time to make friends'. In the Caribbean, you certainly made more than a few friends."

**Trinidad Express,
Trinidad and Tobago**

MOMENTS ...

SURPRISE: After the match between Spain and Saudi-Arabia, a young wild boar created a lot of excitement. It had smuggled itself past the FIFA ticket inspectors without permission and had gained access to the VIP area without accreditation. The fire department caught the young boar, and a veterinarian took care of the animal, which had an injury on his hind leg. Unfortunately, the injured pig, for which the World Cup Office had already been looking for a name, had to be put to sleep a day later.

...

Friday, 23 June 2006
Saudi-Arabia – Spain 0:1

The 1:0 success of Spain over Saudi-Arabia almost became a secondary event on 23 June. On the one hand, the Spanish king Juan Carlos and his wife Sofia were sitting in the stands, on the other hand, rumors were circulating in the arena even before the match started that pop star Robbie Williams was on his way to the stadium. However, the seat, which had indeed been reserved for the world-renowned star, remained unoccupied for 90 minutes.

Gillette
PHILIPS
sense and simplicity
Bud
MILANO
POT
Italia facci

Monday, 26 June 2006
Italy – Australia 1:0

The finale of the five World Cup matches in Kaiserslautern was the encounter between Italy and Australia in the round of sixteen on 26 June. The brave Australians lost in the fifth minute of overtime due to a highly contested penalty – kicked by Francesco Totti – with 0:1. The neutral spectators mourned this injustice together with the Australians. For Italy, it was the first big step on the way to their fourth World Cup win.

(9) TONI Luca
BUFFON Gianluigi
(5) CANNAVARO Fabio
(21) PIRLO Andrea
(7) DEL PIERO Alessandro
(10) TOTTI Francesco
Coach Marcello Lippi

MOMENTS ...

WHEN TWO AUSTRALIAN fans left Fritz-Walter-Stadion with tears in their eyes after the unlucky elimination from the round of sixteen against Italy, an Italian restaurant owner was moved so much that he spontaneously invited the couple to his restaurant. The owner has had his restaurant in Steinstraße for several decades already – but rarely before did a pizza need to offer as much comfort as on that night.

QUOTE ...

"I HAVE NOW been to Munich and Berlin already, and I can only say that Kaiserslautern as the smallest World Cup Host City can measure up very well to the large ones."

Horst Eckel,
World Cup Champion of 1954 and World Cup Ambassador of the city of Kaiserslautern

The big party

It was not only soccer which attracted the masses to Kaiserslautern. More than 600 individual events were offered by the city of Kaiserslautern during the World Cup. From street theater via marching bands to rock concerts with stars such as The BossHoss, Klaus Doldinger's Passport, Revolverheld, Los Paraguayos, Allee der Kosmonauten, or Judy Bailey. The highlight of this entertainment program was the performance of the German-Irish group Reamonn: more than 15.000 visitors crowded Stiftsplatz and the surrounding areas.

Another thing will surely remain unforgettable for visitors: the colorful happenings on the World Cup Mile. The two public viewing places on Barbarossastraße (2,500 people) and on Stiftsplatz (5,000) were connected by a "good mood street". Musicians, artists, and food stands were strung all along the street; fans from very different countries became friends. The city council should consider renaming Eisenbahnstraße, maybe giving it a slightly more cheerful name. Wouldn't that be an idea?

Soccer Fever: The big party
52

SWR
LOTTO
HORST ECKEL
HYUNDAI
SWR
SWR
HYUNDAI
HYUNDAI
MEETING POINT
Football fever.
Priceless.
MasterCard

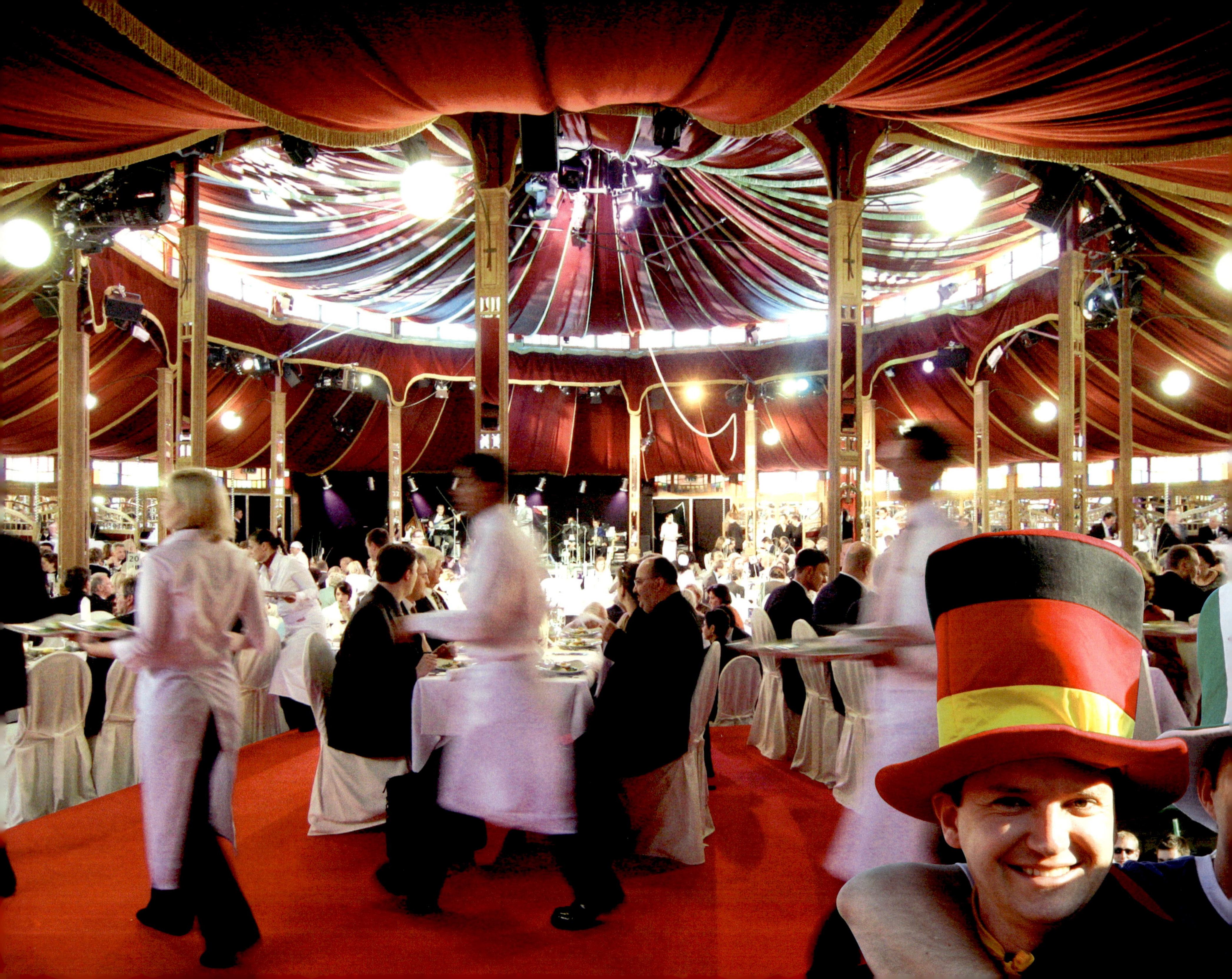

The big party

The entertainment program offered something for every taste: Be it the World Cup Concert with Anna Maria Kaufmann and Xavier Naidoo, the KultTour with Thomas Anders or the World Cup Musical Abydos at the Pfalztheater, Patrick Nuo or "We will rock" on the Stiftsplatz stage, the Helmnot Theater or the carnival parade from Trinidad and Tobago. There were rope-skipping actions of the Kaiserslautern schools, soccer tournaments, and even a City Run to honor Fritz Walter. At the Kammgarn Cultural Center, the musical "pre-games" of the teams playing in Kaiserslautern took place, the Theodor Zink Museum offered a look at the history of sports clothing with its exhibit "Jersey, shirt, and pants", at the Pfalzgalerie, there was an exhibit under the motto "Fascination Soccer", and at the Pfalztheater, one could not only admire soccer-playing robot dogs, but also a Lego model of Fritz-Walter-Stadion consisting of more than one million blocks.

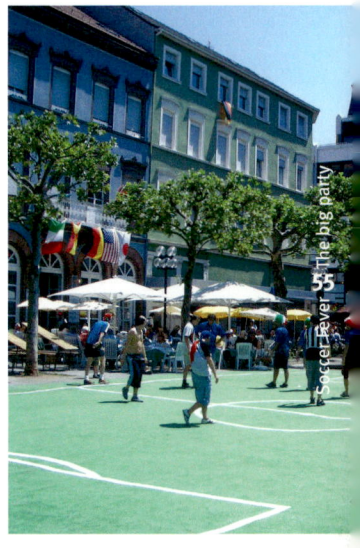

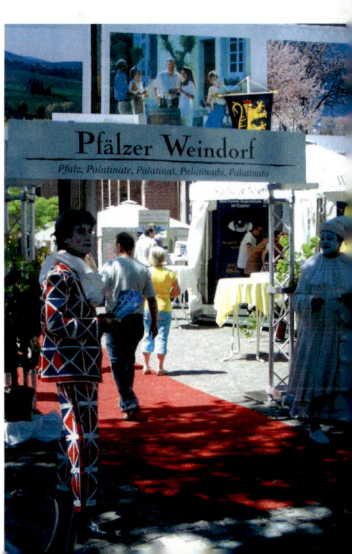

But man does not only live on culture. Colorful and varied was also the multitude of food and drinks being offered, from the dinner show "Salto Culinare" in a mirror tent on Alter Theaterplatz, via the cozy Wine Village of the Palatinate District Association on the inner courtyard of Stiftskirche, to the Fritz Walter Regulars' Table and the numerous stands on the World Cup Mile: There was something for everybody.

Soccer Fever The big party

56

Soccer Fever 57 The big party

The big party

They could not be overheard or overlooked. And this was good. Numerous street artists provided great entertainment to the World Cup visitors with a colorful and varied program. Marching bands, fire-eaters, belly dancers, acrobats – there was something for everyone! Colorful, melodious – and often of high artistic quality. The street became a stage. And Kaiserslautern enchanted its guests.

QUOTE ...

"KAISERSLAUTERN IS alive – and it is more beautiful than ever. Hard to believe how much quality of life this city has gained during the past few months, thanks to the World Cup, if nothing else. Keep it up!"

Karsten,
from Kaiserslautern in the city's Internet guestbook

Soccer Fever The big party 59

Soccer Fever | The big party
60

61 Soccer Fever | The big party

Soccer Fever - The big party
62

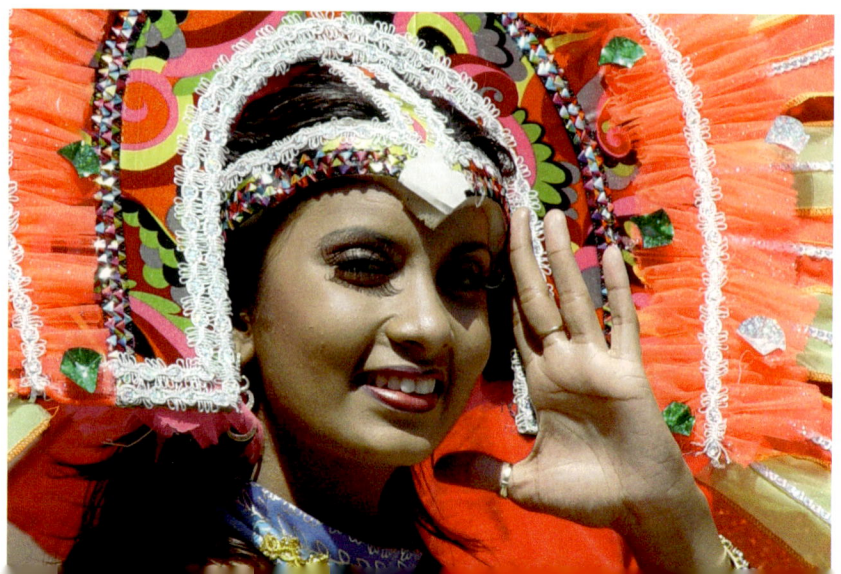

The big party

More than 25,000 spectators lined the fan mile when the carnival street parade from Trinidad and Tobago made its way through the masses of people starting from Stiftsplatz. A lindworm consisting of drummers, fantasy beings, paradise birds, blue devils, stilt walkers, and exotic beauties brought Caribbean flair into the World Cup host city. And somehow it seemed as though everyone got infected by this easygoingness. Even from far away, the rhythms of the different percussion instruments made the visitors dance.

Soccer Fever 64 The big party

The big party

That the Fritz Walter Regulars' Table in front of Stiftskirche would turn out to be the most popular party zone of the entire city could not be predicted. But fans will celebrate where the best atmosphere is – and where the beer supply is assured. Music boomed from the loudspeakers, fans danced on the benches, and yet, despite all this exuberance, it was something that touched even those who hate parties. And let's be honest: When thousands of Australian fans celebrate "Down under" at night in front of the illuminated Stiftskirche church, even the neutral observer may allow himself to be touched.

VOICES ...

"100.000 CITIZENS gave up their German citizenship yesterday – they had no other choice. A crowd of 10,000 Socceroo fans invaded downtown Kaiserslautern around 11 a.m. Within minutes, they had taken over bars, shops, and streets; the city was bathed in yellow and green. St.-Martinsplatz was occupied by so many Australians that it resembled the Australian 'Martin Square' at the best hour of the night."

The Daily Telegraph, Australia

Soccer Fever   The big party
66

The big party

The entire downtown area was turned into a party zone. Between the two public viewing places, there were stand-up stages and pavilions offering regional and international specialties. The people got so used to strolling along the event mile every night, that they almost begged the organizers not to tear it down. Or at least another World Cup Mile, whatever it might be called then, should be set up soon. Could there be a greater compliment?!

MOMENTS ...

ON THE SECOND World Cup day, a house-high fountain was bubbling on Raiffeisenplatz. What visitors first considered a spectacular production and part of the extensive entertainment program, rewarding it with the appropriate applause, was the result of a small accident: A driver had rammed a fire hydrant.

The big party

By the way: The most popular photo subject (in addition to police officers) turned out to be not only the "Eleven Friends" and the three fans sitting high up on the wall at the Löwenburgkreisel traffic circle, but particularly the ten concrete soccer players on Philipp-Mees-Platz. Wearing the shirts of the teams hosted in Kaiserslautern, the figures from the workshop of artist Christel Lechner became magnets for the visitors. And they became the "patron saints" of fans camping without permits.

Soccer Fever – The big party 69

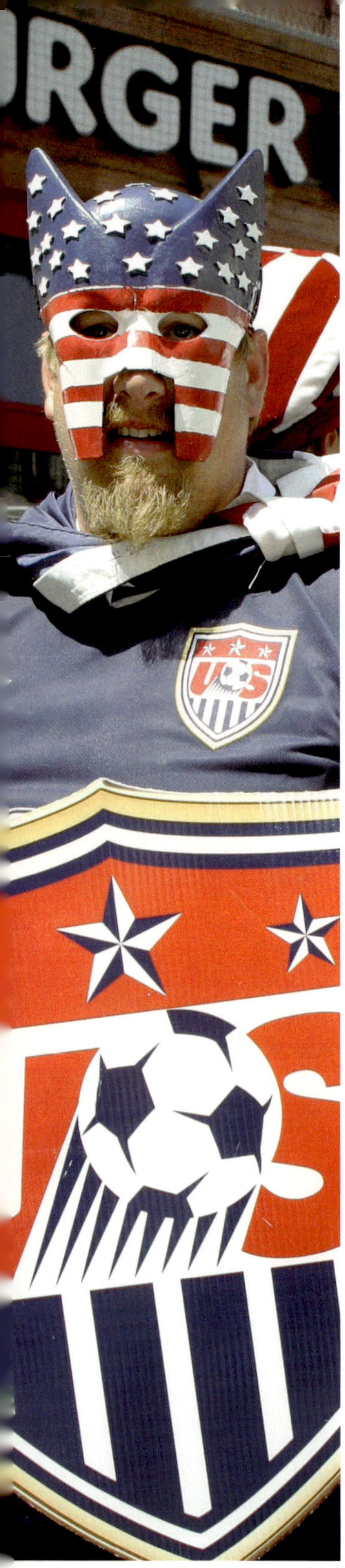
URGER

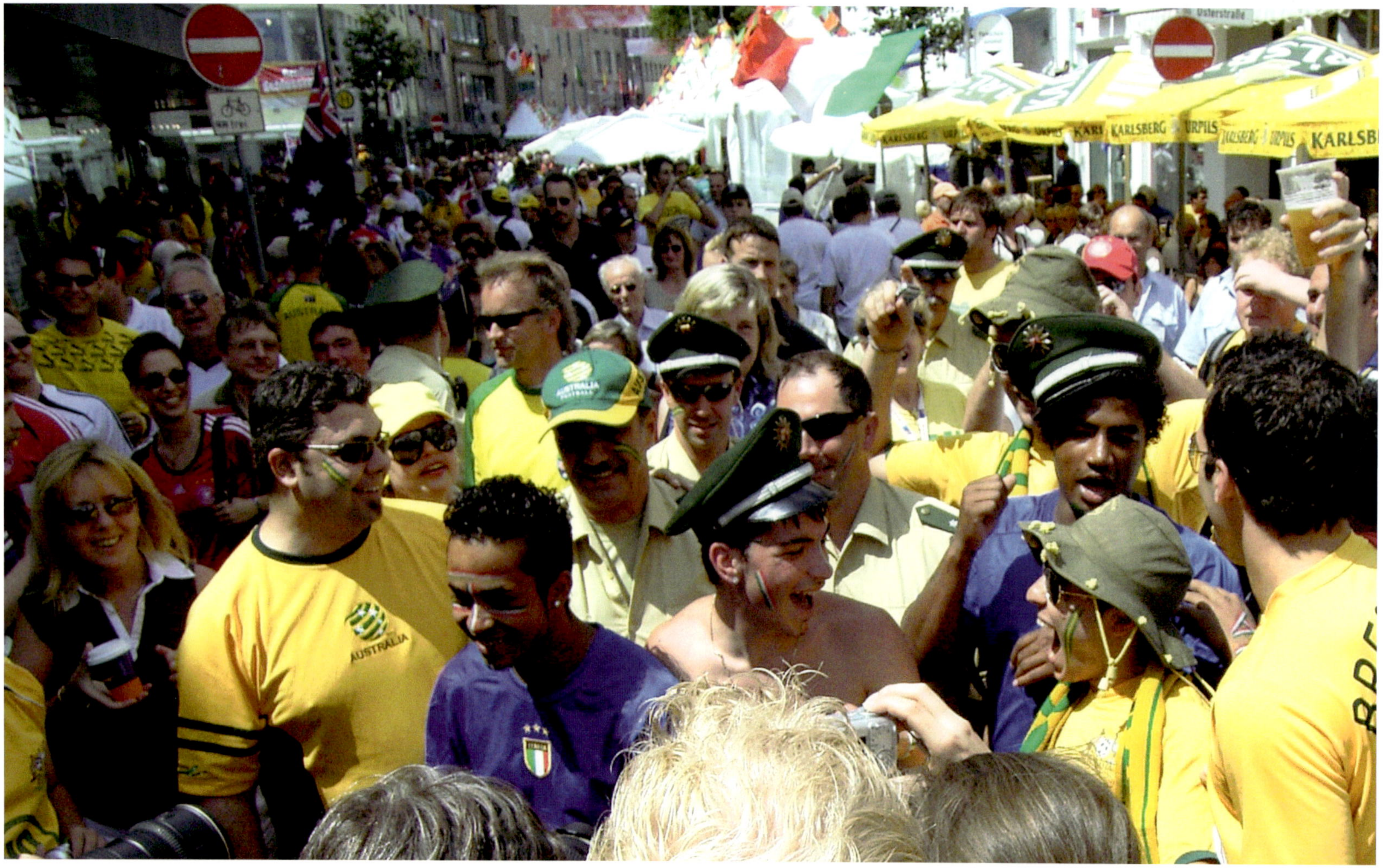
KARLSBERG
AUSTRALIA

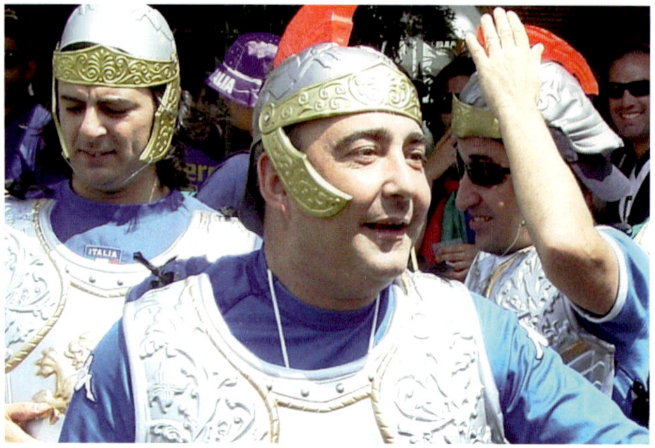

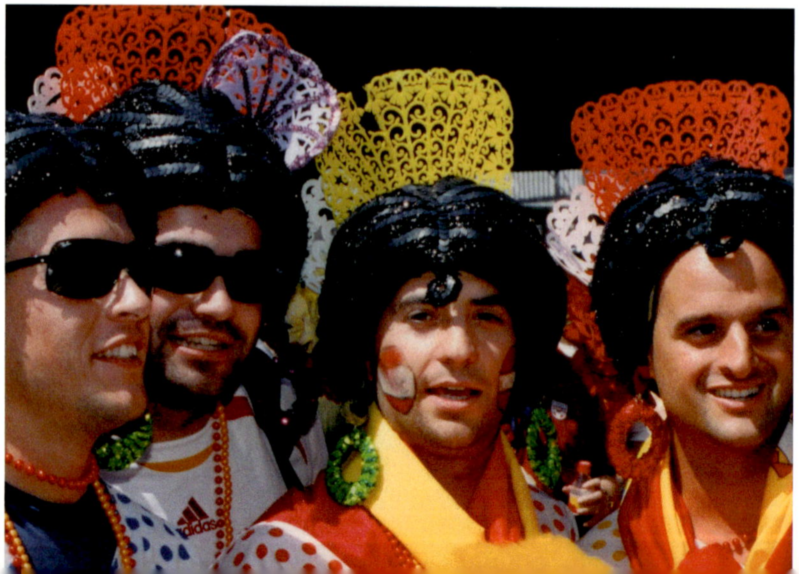

Encounters

Encounters

Unexpected acquaintance: One morning, three Mexicans camping in the old town area rang the door bell at the home of a 40-year-old citizen of Kaiserslautern and asked whether they could take a shower. They could.

Such encounters and similar ones characterized the interaction of residents and guests during the World Cup. The citizens of Kaiserslautern, totally underestimated in their role as hosts, opened their hearts – and their bedrooms. When a young couple asked someone how to get to the fan camp, this person invited the guests to spend the night at his apartment.

Another couple from Kaiserslautern reports that during the World Cup, they became friends with fans from Trinidad and Tobago. A few weeks later the couple from Kaiserslautern already visited their new acquaintances in the Caribbean; more meetings have already been arranged.

It may sound like a modern fairy tale. But residents and guests infected each other with their congeniality. There was no place for bad feelings; openness and trust characterized the encounters. The city with its guests became one large family.

New friendships beyond cultural and national borders have been established. And many contacts will last beyond the World Cup. The World Cup has been worth it. Most certainly.

Soccer Fever Encounters 73

QUOTE ...

"EVERYTHING FIT. At the Fan Fests, different races and religions were standing next to each other. This is how God imagines the world to be, even if we are still 100,000 years away from this in reality."

Franz Beckenbauer, *President of the German World Cup Organizing Committee*

Diary

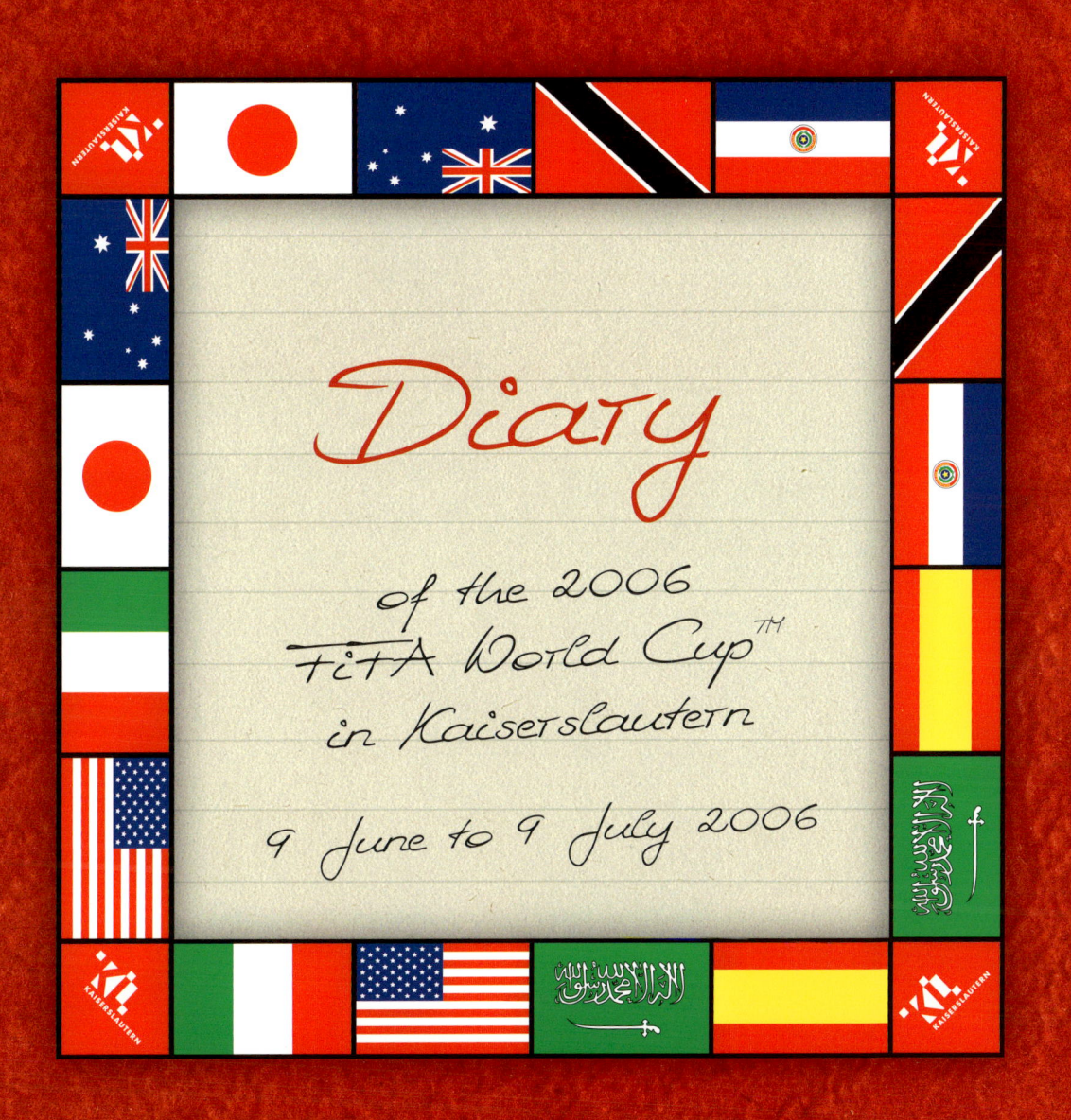

of the 2006 FIFA World Cup™ in Kaiserslautern

9 June to 9 July 2006

Friday, 9 June

Kick-off. At 5.07 p.m., Lord Mayor Bernhard J. Deubig officially opens the World Cup in Kaiserslautern. His dream finals: Germany against the USA. Several tens of thousands of fans are celebrating a peaceful and colorful festival. On the squares and in the downtown area, about 20,000 people are watching the opening match between Germany and Costa Rica. The show "Around the world" performed by the Helmnot Theater exudes elegance and acrobatics. A perfect beginning.

The party can start.

25°C
77°F

Here we go...

Go, Germany, go, score another goal...

Fans from all over the world came to Kaiserslautern.

The band "Grossstadtgeflüster"

Gee whiz: Were those giant ants?

A feeling like in the South: Great atmosphere in the Palatinate Wine Village

FIFA WORLD CUP GERMANY 2006

Destination Germany

Events on this day

- Street Theater Festival, World Cup Mile
  Grotest Maru, La Clique sur Mer, Irrwisch, Cie. d'Outre Rue, Les Bons Enfants
- approx. 1 to 4.45 p.m., Stiftsplatz
  K-Town WM-Band – Great sound from pop to rock
- 1 to 6 p.m., Schillerplatz
  Skiffle Tigers – Marching band
- 3 to 6 p.m., World Cup Mile
  KL WM Jam Band, Esprit – Marching bands
- 4 to 6 p.m., Fan Garden
  Willy-Miller-Band – Disco Funk Soul
- ⚽ 6 p.m., FAN FEST Public Viewing
  Germany : Costa Rica (4:2)
- 7 p.m. to 12 a.m., Schillerplatz
  Esprit – Marching band
- 8 to 9 p.m., Fan Garden
  Grossstadtgeflüster – The not so quiet duo from Berlin
- ⚽ 9 p.m., FAN FEST Public Viewing
  Poland : Ecuador (0:2)
- 11 to 11.25 p.m., Stiftsplatz
  The opening highlight: Helmnot Theater, "Around the World"
- 11 p.m. to 1 a.m., Stiftsplatz
  Brass Machine – Say NO to sampled horns
- 11 p.m. to 1 a.m., Fan Garden
  Dr. Piper – ...may ROCK be with you...

■ ■ ■

Helmnot Theater

Saturday, 10 June

The World Cup Office draws first consequences: Toilet facilities are moved. Everything must fit, so that whatever goes in from the top can also come out at the bottom again.
Three matches live with tropical temperatures. The World Cup becomes a battle in the heat. The ball is also rolling inside the Fruchthalle: Summer Ball of the university and the city.
Elegant suits instead of fan clothing.

81°F ☀ 27°C

It is sooo hot, any refreshment is welcome.

Horst Eckel

The street theater acrobats were the cause of much enjoyment.

We are Germany!

Events on this day

- Street Theater Festival, World Cup Mile
  Grotest Maru, La Clique sur Mer, Irrwisch, Mowetz, Cie. d'Outre Rue, Les Bons Enfants
- approx. 1 to 2.15 p.m., Stiftsplatz
  K-Town WM-Band – Great sound from pop to rock
- 1 to 4 p.m., Fan Garden
  MV Schneckenhausen – Music for the world
- 1 to 5 p.m., World Cup Mile
  Rentnerband, Blaskreis Grün Weiß – Marching bands
- ⚽ 3 p.m., FAN FEST Public Viewing
  England : Paraguay (1:0)
- 5 to 7 p.m., Fan Garden
  Downwind – Classic Rock & more
- ⚽ 6 to 7.45 p.m., FAN FEST Public Viewing
  Trinidad & Tobago : Sweden (0:0)
- 7 to 11 p.m., WM-Meile
  Der Hausfreund, KL WM Jam Band – Marching
- 8 p.m., Fruchthalle
  University Summer Ball
- 8 p.m. to 12 a.m., Fan Garden
  Dr. Detroit & the JB Horns – Make it funky
- ⚽ 9 p.m., FAN FEST Public Viewing
  Argentina : Ivory Coast (2:1)
- 11 p.m. to 1 a.m., Stiftsplatz
  K-Town Allstars – feat. Stephan Flesch and other well-known musicians

■ ■ ■

University Summer Ball at Fruchthalle

…y Summer Ball

Sunday, 11 June

First of four Sundays on which stores were open for business. Young people from the partner city Bunkyo-ku and from Kaiserslautern compete in a football match. State and city hold a reception at the Fruchthalle. Minister President Kurt Beck, who just had to shake many hundreds of hands in the pedestrian zone, DFB President Dr. Theo Zwanziger, and FIFA Vice-President Ismail Bhamjee from Botswana praise the friendliness of the people of Kaiserslautern. Bhamjee must leave Germany a few days later, because he sold tickets on the black market.

Over-sized jersey of the Japanese national team on the grounds of the Japanese Garden. Visitors could sign it.

79°F

26°C

Street artists

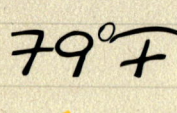

A city full of people

La Clique sur Mer

Events on this day

- Street Theater Festival, World Cup Mile
  Grotest Maru, La Clique sur Mer, Irrwisch, Mowetz, Cie. d'Outre Rue, Les Bons Enfants
- approx. 1 to 2.15 p.m., Stiftsplatz
  K-Town WM-Band
- 1 to 3 p.m., Fan Garden
  Pfälzer Konzert-Blasorchester – Musikverein Rodenbach
- 1 to 5 p.m., World Cup Mile
  Blaskreis Grün Weiß, All that Jazz – Marching bands
- ⚽ 3 p.m., FAN FEST Public Viewing
  Serbia & Montenegro : Netherlands (0:1)
- 4 to 8 p.m., Schillerplatz
  Der Hausfreund – Marching band
- 5 to 7 p.m., Fan Garden
  Nimm 2 – Piano pop and swing rarities
- ⚽ 6 p.m., FAN FEST Public Viewing
  Mexico : Iran (3:1)
- 7 to 11 p.m., World Cup Mile
  Esprit, Acoustical Jam – Marching bands
- 8 p.m. to 12 a.m., Fan Garden
  is' was – Oldies & Rock
- ⚽ 9 p.m., FAN FEST Public Viewing
  Angola : Portugal (0:1)
- 11 to 12 a.m., Stiftsplatz
  K-Town WM-Band – Great sound from pop to rock
- 11 to 11.10 p.m., Stiftsplatz
  Helmnot-Theater, "Windriders"

The smile is still a little reserved...

This is how the Portuguese celebrated.

at Fruchthalle

Minister President Kurt Beck and Lord Mayor Bernhard J. Deubig

Monday, 12 June

84°F 29°C

The first Australian football fans already arrive in the morning. Restaurant owners get ready for the invasion. First official reception of the Lord Mayor with the Australian ambassador and the Japanese consul general. German TV station ZDF broadcasts its noon magazine live from Kaiserslautern. About 80,000 visitors are counted in the context of the first game between Japan and Australia. First stress test is passed with flying colors. Don't even think of sleep today.

Australia's first World Cup victory in history: The fifth continent is celebrating in Kaiserslautern.

2006 FIFA World Cup Germany™

12 AUSTRALIA - JAPAN

Group F - Fritz-Walter-Stadion - Kaiserslautern - 12 June 2006
Kick-off: 15:00 hrs

Stadionbetreiber | Fritz-Walter-Stadion
0000000828

- BLUE SECTOR -
Osttribüne

Block: **18.1**   Row: **19**   Seat: **7**

Group F
12

Gilt am Spieltag als Fahrausweis zur Benutzung aller Verkehrsmittel (2. Klasse) im WVV, VRN, RNN, VGS, VRT, VRM.

Includes free use of all local public transport (2nd class) on match day within the WVV, VRN, RNN, VGS, VRT, VRM.

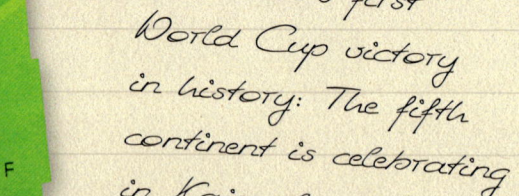

Ticket beinhaltet Chip – bitte nicht knicken oder beschädigen.
Ticket contains a chip – please do not fold or puncture.

FIFAworldcup.com   FIFA

0041242666059003606005100

02.05.06
02:05 hrs
18.1/19/7

Carefully optimistic...

Sure of victory!

Just cute: Goleo and Japanese fans

Jubilant.

Go Aussi Go!!!

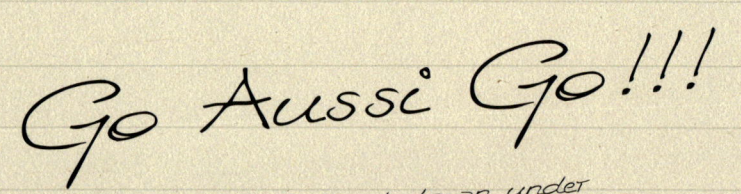

*"I come from a land down under
Where beer does flow and men chunder
Can't you hear, can't you hear the thunder?
You better run, you better take cover..."*

Fritz-Walter Stammtisch

GO SOCCEROOS!

www.footballaustralia.com.au

AUSTRALIA

世界よ来たれ、
友のもとへ

Feeling like partying despite the defeat.

Events on this day

- Street Theater Festival, World Cup Mile
  Grotest Maru, La Clique sur Mer, Irrwisch, Mowetz, Cie. d'Outre Rue, Les Bons Enfants
- approx. 1 to 2.15 p.m., Stiftsplatz
  Giovanni Contrino – ... the Italian decision
- 1 to 3 p.m. and 5 to 6 p.m. World Cup Mile
  Der Hausfreund, KL WM Jam Band – Marching bands
- 1 to 3 p.m. and 5 to 8 p.m., Schillerplatz
  Lulu Weiss Ensemble – Marching band
- 1 to 3 p.m., Fan Garden
  Tommy H. Price – Songwriting: American pop & rock music
- ⚽ 3 p.m., FAN FEST Public Viewing and stadium
  Australia : Japan (3:1)
- 5 to 7 p.m., Fan Garden
  Colorful – Trendy folk rock
- ⚽ 6 p.m., FAN FEST Public Viewing
  USA : Czech Republic (0:3)
- 8 p.m. to 12 a.m., Fan Garden
  Elliot – Feel the cover
- ⚽ 9 p.m., FAN FEST Public Viewing
  Italy : Ghana (2:0)
- 11 p.m. to 1 a.m., Stiftsplatz
  Rob Tognoni – Power blues rock

AFTERMATCH PARTY
12. 06. –
Start ° 11:00 pm °
°resident djs°
S.GROOVESCHARNIER
°hertzmusic.com | hertzclub°
DANIEL R.
°twenty one resident°

21 twenty one
lounge · café bar · deli-resto

Tuesday, 13 June

Kaiserslautern is sleeping in today. Still, 20,000 visitors again invade the city. Press conference in the city hall's great chamber: Police and city report positive results so far. And present a birthday cake to the Lord Mayor, who is celebrating his 58th birthday today. The hotels are all fully booked. The private accommodation service is also well received. Top favorite Brazil enters into the tournament. Although it is his birthday, the Lord Mayor goes to the hospital to pay a visit to a Japanese reporter, who had severely injured himself on a kids' slide during a recording session. Crazy World Cup!

Happy Birthday, Bernie!

Wenn die Welt kommt, mach ich ihr das Bett.

Elsa

Machen Sie mit! „Private Bettenbörse" zur FIFA WM 2006™

88°F
31°C

Australian-style sunscreen.

Communication is going well

Beautifulll...

Buddy buddies.

... and two exotic beauties.

Events on this day

- Street Theater Festival, World Cup Mile
  Grotest Maru, La Clique sur Mer, Cie. d'Outre Rue, Les Bons Enfants
- approx. 1 to 1.45 p.m., Stiftsplatz
  K-Town WM-Band – Great sound from pop to rock
- 1 to 3 p.m. and 5 to 6 p.m., World Cup Mile
  Esprit, KL WM Jam Band – Marching bands
- approx. 2 to 2.15 p.m., Stiftsplatz
  VIVA Brasil Samba Dance Show
- 2 to 4 p.m., Fan Garden
  Rittersberg Big Band – Swing at the Fan Garden
- ⚽ 3 p.m., FAN FEST Public Viewing
  South Korea : Togo (2:1)
- 6 to 6.30 p.m., Fan Garden
  VIVA Brasil Samba Dance Show
- ⚽ 6 p.m., FAN FEST Public Viewing
  France : Switzerland (0:0)
- 8 p.m. to 12 a.m., Fan Garden
  Favorits – The Kaiserslautern Dance Band
- ⚽ 9 p.m., FAN FEST Public Viewing
  Brazil : Croatia (1:0)
- 11 p.m. to 1 a.m., Stiftsplatz
  K-Town WM-Band – Great sound from pop to rock

Wednesday, 14 June

The city's public order office is proud to announce: "Glass free" has indeed been realized! That evening, 40,000 fans watch the match of the German national team against Poland in the city. Goosebump feeling: The Queen cover band "The Great Pretender" celebrates with the German fans: "We are the champions".

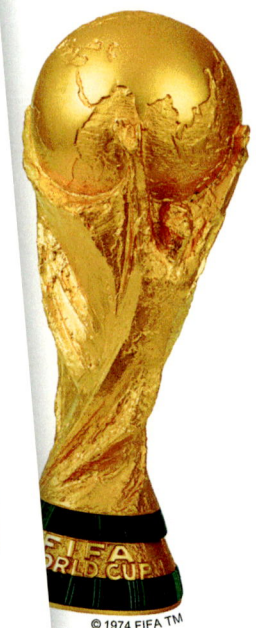

90°F 32°C

A peck on the cheek...

Kaiserslautern is celebrating "glass free"

"We are the champions!"

Second match, second victory

The Great Pretender

Events on this day

- Street Theater Festival, World Cup Mile
  Grotest Maru, La Clique sur Mer, Irrwisch, Cie. d'Outre Rue, Les Bons Enfants
- approx. 1 to 2.15 p.m., Stiftsplatz
  K-Town WM-Band – Great sound from pop to rock
- 1 to 3 p.m., Fan Garden
  Pfalzband Niederkirchen – Modern dance & mood music
- 1 to 3 p.m. and 5 to 6 p.m., World Cup Mile
  KL WM Jam Band, Blaskreis Grün Weiß – Marching bands
- ⚽ 3 p.m., FAN FEST Public Viewing
  Spain : Ukraine (4:0)
- 1 to 6 p.m., Fan Garden
  Acoustical Jam – The new sound
- 5 to 9 p.m., Schillerplatz
  REHA Ensemble – Marching band
- ⚽ 6 p.m., FAN FEST Public Viewing
  Tunisia : Saudi-Arabia (2:2)
- 7 to 9 p.m., Fan Garden
  Deafen Goblins – Party pur
- ⚽ 9 p.m., FAN FEST Public Viewing
  Germany : Poland (1:0)
- 11 p.m. to 1 a.m., Stiftsplatz
  The Great Pretender – Die Queen Music Show
- 11 p.m. to 12 a.m., Fan Garden
  Deafen Goblins – Nothing but party
- ■ ■ ■

Street theater
Cie. d'Outre Rue in the
pedestrian zone

Thursday, 15 June

Holiday. And yet, 10,000 people come to the city. The first fans from Italy and the USA arrive. In the meantime, Australians have extended their stay in Kaiserslautern. Because it is nice to stay with us.

28°C
82°F

Events on this day

- Street Theater Festival, World Cup Mile
  Grotest Maru, Irrwisch
- approx. 1 to 2.15 p.m., Stiftsplatz
  K-Town WM-Band – Great sound from pop to rock
- 1 to 3 p.m., Fan Garden
  MV Otterberg – Concert-style entertainment music
- 1 to 3 p.m. and 5 to 6 p.m., World Cup Mile
  Esprit, KL WM Jam Band – Marching bands
- 3 p.m., FAN FEST Public Viewing
  Ecuador : Costa Rica (3:0)
- 6 p.m., FAN FEST Public Viewing
  England : Trinidad & Tobago (2:0)
- 6 p.m. to 12 a.m., Fan Garden
  Undercover – Mission to Rock – The Southwestern Palatinate's party rock band
- 8 p.m., Pfalztheater
  Rock Opera Abydos – Powerful audiovisual stage spectacle
- 9 p.m., FAN FEST Public Viewing
  Sweden : Paraguay (1:0)
- 11 p.m. to 1 a.m., Stiftsplatz
  ABBA da capo – The ABBA Revival Show

Put on your dancing shoes

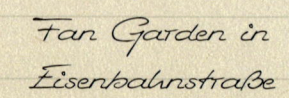

…up, and away…

Fan Garden in Eisenbahnstraße

77°F  25°C

Friday, 16 June

The calm before the storm. The city's homepage gets top ratings from the tourism magazine FVW: Detailed, sufficient information, simple navigation. Check Six and Touch'n Go are competing with Angola, Mexico and Ivory Coast for the favor of the visitors. In the Pfalztheater, a "duel" is on between Xavier Naidoo and Anna Maria Kaufmann: "You'll never walk alone".

Events on this day

- Street Theater Festival, World Cup Mile
  Les Frites Foutues, Mabó Band, Les Obsessionelles, Glücksstück
- approx. 1 to 2.15 p.m., Stiftsplatz
  Eddie St. James & Band – Pop/Rock with Californian Sound
- 1 to 3 p.m., Fan Garden
  UNI Big Band – Swing, Latin & Funk
- 1 to 3 p.m. and 5 to 6 p.m., World Cup Mile
  KL WM Jam Band, Der Hausfreund – Marching bands
- ⚽ 5 p.m., FAN FEST Public Viewing
  Argentina : Serbia & Montenegro (6:0)
- 3 to 7 p.m., Schillerplatz
  Blaskreis Grün Weiß Latin – Marching band
- 4 to 6 p.m., Fan Garden
  Crime & Passion – Simply acoustic
- ⚽ 6 p.m., FAN FEST Public Viewing
  Netherlands : Ivory Coast (2:1)
- 7 to 9 p.m., Fan Garden
  Check Six – Big Band Formation of the USAFE Band
- 8 p.m., Pfalztheater
  The World Football Concerts – From opera via musical to pop music
- ⚽ 9 p.m., FAN FEST Public Viewing
  Mexico : Angola (0:0)
- 10 p.m. to 12 a.m., Fan Garden
  Touch'n Go – The Rock Formation of the USAFE Band
- 11 p.m. to 1 a.m., Stiftsplatz
  los Santanos – Tribute to Santana – Latinrock

„Und wenn ein Lied meine Lippen verlässt…"
("And when a song leaves my lips…")

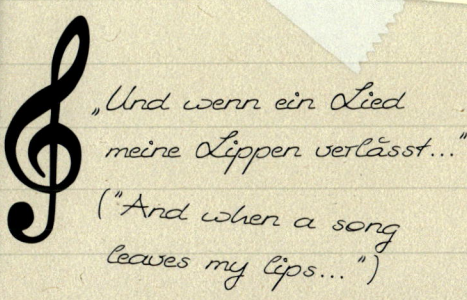

Saturday, 17 June

Fourth anniversary of the death of Fritz Walter: In Alsenborn, a statue is unveiled in the presence of numerous guests of honor; before the game, a minute of silence is observed in "his" stadium. The city had fought for this for a long time.

At the Media Point, the ambassadors of Italy and the USA hold a joint press conference with the Lord Mayor. Even CNN reports. More than 100,000 fans come to the city and to the stadium. The Public Viewing places must be blocked off three hours before the start of the match. FIFA President Joseph S. Blatter and OC Chairman Franz Beckenbauer sit in the stands. Visitor record at the fan camp: More than 1,100 guests are counted.

U.S. Ambassador William R. Timken jr. and his wife Susan at the World Cup Cafe

79°F
26°C

Fritz Walter – God of Football!
Now he has a monument in Alsenborn.

Franz Beckenbauer gives an autograph to "World Cup Grandma Elsa"

2006 FIFA World Cup Germany™

25 **ITALY – USA**

Group E · Fritz-Walter-Stadion · Kaiserslautern · 17 June 2006
Kick-off: 21:00 hrs

Host City | Kaiserslautern
Edgar Gerhards

– YELLOW SECTOR –
Westtribüne

Block: **9.1**   Row: **18**   Seat: **25**

A minute of silence for Fritz Walter

Forza Italia!

Go, USA, go!

Absolutely crazy! So many people...

Closed due to overcrowding

1:1

two yellow cards

Gotcha!

Did you see everything?

Events on this day

- Street Theater Festival, World Cup Mile
  Les Frites Foutues, Mabó Band, Glücksstück
- approx. 1 to 2.15 p.m., Stiftsplatz
  Live Act Trinidad & Tobago
- 1 to 3 p.m., Fan Garden
  MV Otterbach – Westpfälzer Blasorchester
- 1 to 5 p.m., World Cup Mile
  Acoustical Jam, KL WM Jam Band – Marching bands
- 1 to 6 p.m., Schillerplatz
  Der Hausfreund – Marching band
- ⚽ 3 p.m., FAN FEST Public Viewing
  Portugal : Iran (2:0)
- 4 to 7 p.m., Fan Garden
  Wet Desert – Power pop with violin
- ⚽ 6 p.m., FAN FEST Public Viewing
  Czech Republic : Ghana (0:2)
- 7 to 9 p.m., Schillerplatz
  New Orleans Shufflers – Marching band
- 7 to 9 p.m., World Cup Mile
  Der Hausfreund, KL WM Jam Band, USAFE Marching band – Marching bands
- 8 to 9 p.m., Fan Garden
  Horizon – The unique Italo-pop band
- ⚽ 9 p.m., FAN FEST Public Viewing and stadium
  Italy : USA (1:1)
- 11 p.m. to 1 a.m. Stiftsplatz
  Bongiovio – The !! Tribute to Bon Jovi
- 11 p.m. to 1 a.m., Fan Garden
  Horizon – The unique Italo-pop band
- ...

Would also like to sleep in on a bed of roses some day...

K-Town rocks!

Sunday, 18 June

Kaiserslautern is holding siesta. After a long night, it was time to take a deep breath. The outdoor swimming pools, on the other hand, enjoy a record number of visitors.
Swimming instead of football. Still, the people of Kaiserslautern and their guests celebrate: 20,000 people on a "normal" day.

88°F
31°C

"Glücksstück"

Refreshing

Events on this day

- Street Theater Festival, World Cup Mile
  Le SNOB, Les Frites Foutues, Les Obsessionelles, Glücksstück
- approx. 1 to 2.15 p.m., Stiftsplatz
  DJ-Party
- 1 to 3 p.m., Fan Garden
  MV Mackenbach – Music is in the air
- 1 to 5 p.m., World Cup Mile
  Chicago Bounce, Red Hot Dixie Devils – Marching bands
- 2 to 6 p.m., Schillerplatz
  Acoustical Jam – Marching band
- ⚽ 3 p.m., FAN FEST Public Viewing
  Japan : Croatia (0:0)
- 3.30 p.m., Training camp of 1. FCK, Fröhnerhof
  National team of Germany's top chefs : 1. FCK traditional team (4:19)
  Juicy match with subsequent gala in the mirror tent
- 5 to 7 p.m., Fan Garden
  Rhumba Kartell – The swing of life –
  Swing of the 1930s & 1940s
- ⚽ 6 p.m., FAN FEST Public Viewing
  Brazil : Australia (2:0)
- 7 p.m. to 12 a.m., World Cup Mile
  KL WM Jam Band, Blaskreis Grün Weiß – Marching bands
- 8 p.m. to 12 a.m., Fan Garden
  40 Years Volker Klimmer Band – The extraordinary show band
- ⚽ 9 p.m., FAN FEST Public Viewing
  France : Republic Korea (1:1)
- 11 p.m. to 12 a.m., Stiftsplatz
  Chill-Out / DJ-Party

Monday, 19 June

FIFA praises the World Cup Office for the efficient workflows during the arrival and departure of the fans. Party on Stiftsplatz: Los Paraguayos, the cult band from Paraguay, creates more enthusiasm than Roque Santa Cruz and his colleagues.

82°F 28°C

The World Cup is omnipresent

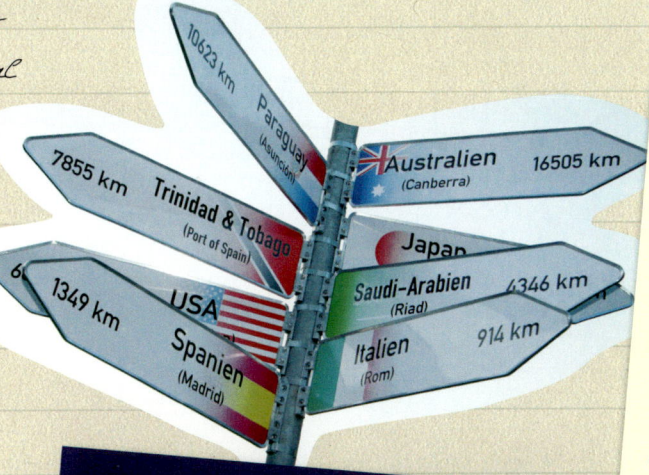

Match No. **53** Kaiserslautern
Car Parking Pass
2720

Events on this day

- Street Theater Festival, World Cup Mile
  Le SNOB, Pas ParTout, Mabó Band, Les Obsessionelles, Glücksstück
- approx. 1 to 2.15 p.m., Stiftsplatz
  K-Town WM-Band – Great sound from pop to rock
- 1 to 3 p.m., Fan Garden
  Stadtkapelle Frankenthal – Mozart, musicals and more
- 1 to 3 p.m. and 5 to 6 p.m., World Cup Mile
  Esprit, KL WM Jam Band – Marching bands
- ⚽ 3 p.m., FAN FEST Public Viewing
  Togo : Switzerland (0:2)
- 4 to 7 p.m., Fan Garden
  Harald Krüger & Walt Bender – Hits and evergreens from seven decades
- 4 to 8 p.m. Schillerplatz
  Lulu Weiss Ensemble – Marching band
- ⚽ 6 p.m., FAN FEST Public Viewing
  Saudi-Arabia : Ukraine (0:4)
- 8 p.m. to 1 a.m., Fan Garden
  JB Project – Brass meets Vocal
- ⚽ 9 p.m., FAN FEST Public Viewing
  Spain : Tunisia (3:1)
- 11 p.m. to 1 a.m., Stiftsplatz
  Los Paraguayos – The cult band from Paraguay

Tuesday, 20 June

Carnival in Trinidad and Tobago. Stop. No. We are in Kaiserslautern. But it feels like the Caribbean. Then Germany against Ecuador. 40,000 fans are cheering because Germany made it into the round of sixteen. The city comes to a standstill. Paraguay and Trinidad and Tobago compete at Fritz-Walter-Stadion. In the end, city and police count 80,000 guests.

77°F
25°C

Am I not beautiful?

Where did all the Indians go?

Go, Roque, go!

Germany on the giant screen!

And we won again…

Events on this day

- Street Theater Festival, World Cup Mile
  Pas ParTout, Mabó Band, Les Obsessionelles, Glücksstück, Cie. Colbok

- 12 to 2 p.m., World Cup Mile
  Great Carnival – Parade from Trinidad & Tobago

- approx. 1 to 3.30 p.m., Stiftsplatz
  Straight Ahead – Latin – Swing – Vocals

- 1 to 4 p.m., World Cup Mile
  H. Krüger & Low Budget, Phönix Jazzband – Marching bands

- 1 to 4 p.m., Schillerplatz
  KL WM Jam Band – Marching band

- 1 to 4 p.m., Fan Garden
  Zellertaler Old Brass Band

- ⚽ 4 p.m., FAN FEST Public Viewing
  Ecuador : Germany (0:3)
  Costa Rica : Poland (1:2)

- 5 to 9 p.m., World Cup Mile
  KL WM Jam Band, Jack's Blues Caravane – Marching bands

- 6 to 8.30 p.m., Fan Garden
  Allee der Kosmonauten

- 6 to 9 p.m., Schillerplatz
  Der Hausfreund – Marching band

- 6.30 to 7.15 p.m., Stiftsplatz
  Live Act Trinidad & Tobago

- ⚽ 9 p.m., Fan Fest Public Viewing und Stadion
  Paraguay : Trinidad & Tobago (2:0)
  Sweden : England (2:2)

- 11 p.m. to 1 a.m., Stiftsplatz
  Riddim Posse – Caribbean Party

- 11 p.m. to 1 a.m., Fan Garden
  Rock Marley – Reggae hits with a rock sound

■ ■ ■

Wednesday, 21 June

Flags have disappeared from in front of the Pfalztheater. The World Cup Office appeals to the thieves and asks that they be returned. The K-Town WM Band re-awakens visitors on Stiftsplatz after the match Netherlands against Argentina.

25°C
77°F

Events on this day

- Street Theater Festival, World Cup Mile
  Cie. Colbok
- 1 to 3 p.m., Fan Garden
  Die AG – Andy and Günni of Snailshouse
- approx. 1 to 3.30 p.m., Stiftsplatz
  K-Town WM-Band – Great sound from pop to rock
- 1 to 4 p.m., World Cup Mile
  Jack's Blues Caravane, KL WM Jam Band – Marching bands
- ⚽ 4 p.m., FAN FEST Public Viewing
  Iran : Angola (1:1)
  Portugal : Mexico (2:1)
- 6 to 8 p.m., Fan Garden
  Transonic – No canned music
- 6 to 9 p.m., World Cup Mile
  Esprit, Jack's Blues Caravane – Marching band
- 7.40 to 8.10 p.m., Stiftsplatz
  TC Rot Weiß – Break-dance show
- ⚽ 9 p.m., FAN FEST Public Viewing
  Netherlands : Argentina (0:0)
  Ivory Coast : Serbia & Montenegro (3:2)
- 9 p.m. to 12
  Celebration –
- 11 p.m. to 12
  K-Town WM-B

All of a sudden, the flags were gone!

TC Rot Weiß – Break-dance show

Where is Lehmann? The life-size replica of the national goalkeeper at Schillerplatz has disappeared. The police video camera recording is checked.

Companie Colbok on the World Cup Mile

Thursday, 22 June

1,200 school students dug out a long-forgotten type of sports: rope skipping. "Get fit for 2006!" Call from Trinidad and Tobago: The artists from the Caribbean nation say thanks for the hospitality. In no other city did the citizens wave them good-bye. Great joy in the evening: Italy and Australia qualify themselves for the match of the round of sixteen in Kaiserslautern.

21°C
70°F

Hello Phönix Jazzband…

Jens Lehmann is replaced. Overnight, a new, life-size figure of the German goalkeeper is produced and set up at noon.

We need a sticker. This is the draft (continued on 26 June)

Events on this day

- Street Theater Festival, World Cup Mile
  Cie. Midi 12, BrassBuffet, Cie. Colbok
- Starting at 11 p.m., Fraunhofer Center,
  "365 Landmarks in the Land of Ideas" – Kaiserslautern as an important part of the campaign
- 11 to 11.10 p.m., World Cup Mile
  Rope Skipping – The spectacle
- approx. 1 to 2.15 p.m., Stiftsplatz
  Corruption Airways – Funk & Soul at its best
- 1 to 3 p.m., Fan Garden
  MiCarla – Rhumba, Gitarro, Rock & Flamenco
- 1 to 4 p.m., World Cup Mile
  KL WM Jam Band, Phönix Jazzband – Marching bands
- approx. 2.15 to 3.30 p.m., Stiftsplatz
  Midnight Movers – Playing the classics of soul
- ⚽ 4 p.m., FAN FEST Public Viewing
  Czech Republic : Italy (0:2)
  Ghana : USA (2:1)
- 4 to 6 p.m., Fan Garden
  Petermann's Swing Partie – The Western Palatinate Big Band
- 4 to 8 p.m., Schillerplatz
  Esprit – Marching band
- 6 to 9 p.m., World Cup Mile
  Blaskreis Grün Weiß, H. Krüger
- 7 p.m. to 12 a.m., Fan Garden
  The Ready Teddys – Rock 'n' Roll
- ⚽ 9 p.m., FAN FEST Public Viewing
  Japan : Brazil (1:4)
  Croatia : Australia (2:2)
- 11 p.m. to 12 a.m., Stiftsplatz
  Midnight Movers – Playing the classics of soul

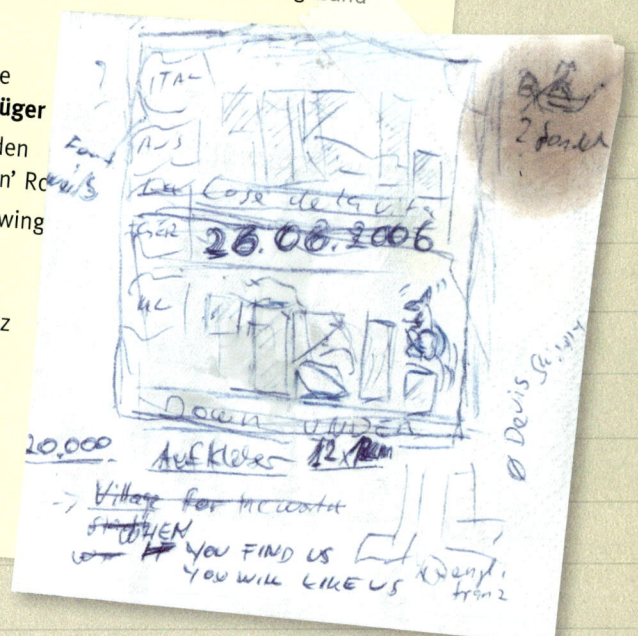

■ ■ ■

BrassBuffet

Friday, 23 June

Live broadcasts from Kaiserslautern on 3 programs of German TV station ARD: Morning Magazine, Brisant, and Noon Magazine. In the meantime, Spanish king Juan Carlos arrives by plane at Ramstein. The Minister President welcomes him; the Lord Mayor does this in the stadium. Spanish and Arabic city volunteers show fans the way to the stadium using megaphones. 80,000 guests are in the city. The actual party only starts after the match of Spain against Saudi-Arabia: Reamonn draws 15,000 enthusiastic fans. Meanwhile, the Media Point is changed into a TV studio at short notice. The two-hour live program of Saudi Sport Channel 3 from Kaiserslautern is watched by 35 million people in the Arab-speaking part of the world.

23°C
73°F

The Minister President welcomes the Spanish king

Great gesture: For the traditional Muslim Friday prayer, two schools, St.-Franziskus-Realschule and -Gymnasium, opened their gyms. 200 prayer carpets were laid out.

Family excursion

This is a sheik.

Spanish Eyes hidden behind glasses.

The original Lehmann is back.

As an investigation by the Kaiserslautern World Cup Office revealed, the replica of Lehmann located at Schillerplatz had been removed by unknown subjects on Tuesday night. In the early morning hours of 21 June, employees of a restaurant picked up the goalkeeper, who had been carelessly left lying on the ground. They report that he very quickly became a part of their team, doing "valuable work" in the kitchen. Only when they read yesterday's media reports, did the restaurant team realize that their kitchen helper was the most-wanted plastic figure in the entire republic. They immediately contacted the city volunteers' drivers on duty, who freed the Arsenal goalkeeper from his kitchen job and gave him a comfortable place to stay in the Kaiserslautern city hall.

23 June

Reamonn is finally here!

Events on this day

- Street Theater Festival, World Cup Mile
  Cia. Sarruga, Cie. Midi 12, BrassBuffet, Cie. Albédo, Cie. d'Outre Rue, Cie. Colbok
- approx. 1 to 3.30 p.m., Stiftsplatz
  K-Town WM-Band – Great sound from pop to rock
- 1 to 4 p.m., World Cup Mile
  Chicago Bounce, KL WM Jam Band – Marching bands
- 1 to 4 p.m., Fan Garden
  Mocabo – Gipsy Guitars, Spanish Songs & Latin Grooves
- 1 to 4 p.m., Schillerplatz
  Blaskreis Grün Weiß Latin – Marching band
- ⚽ 4 p.m., FAN FEST Public Viewing and stadium
  Saudi-Arabia : Spain (0:1)
  Ukraine : Tunisia (1:0)
- 6 to 8.30 p.m., Fan Garden
  Judy Bailey – The sunnygirl from Barbados
- 6 to 9 p.m., World Cup Mile
  Jack's Blues Caravane, Esprit – Marching bands
- 6 to 9 p.m., Schillerplatz
  KL WM Jam Band – Marching band
- 6.30 to 7 p.m., Stiftsplatz
  Feverdog – British rock "without a stuffy nose"
- 7.15 to 7.45 p.m., Stiftsplatz
  Black Phoenix
- 8.15 to 9.30 p.m., Stiftsplatz
  Menschenskinder – Charity project with German and Swiss artists
- 10 to 11.30 p.m., Stiftsplatz
  Reamonn
- ⚽ 9 p.m., FAN FEST Public Viewing
  Togo : France (0:2)
  Switzerland : Republic Korea (2:0)
- 9 p.m. to 12 a.m., Fan Garden
  Harald Krüger & Low Budget – The ultimate Rock 'n' Roll Party

Saturday, 24 June

Once again, 30,000 fans in the city. On an afternoon. Germany wins against Sweden. Things start to become scary.

84°F

29°C

Events on this day

- Street Theater Festival, World Cup Mile
  Cia. Sarruga, Cie. Midi 12, BrassBuffet, Cie. Albédo, Theater Pikante, Cie. Colbok

- 1 to 2.30 p.m., Fan Garden
  Samba Kids – Exciting German percussion group

- approx. 1 to 2.45 p.m., Stiftsplatz
  Booty Jam – Soul funk with a blast

- 1 to 5 p.m., Schillerplatz
  Chicago Bounce – Marching band

- approx. 3 to 4.15 p.m., Stiftsplatz
  Samba Kids – Exciting German percussion group

- 3 to 5 p.m., World Cup Mile
  Phönix Jazzband, All that Jazz – Marching bands

- 4 to 5 p.m., Fan Garden
  Rhythm & Brass Band – The best of rock, pop, soul & funk

- 5 p.m., FAN FEST Public Viewing
  Round of Sixteen – Germany : Sweden (2:0)

- All night long, Fruchthalle and other locations
  The Long Night of Culture – Over 50 different cultural events

- 7 to 9 p.m., World Cup Mile
  KL WM Jam Band, Der Hausfreund – Marching bands

- 7 to 9 p.m., Fan Garden
  Rhythm & Brass Band – The best of rock, pop, soul & funk

- 7.40 to 8.10 p.m., Stiftsplatz
  Shiro Kumo Show Team – Japanese martial arts show

- 9 p.m., FAN FEST Public Viewing
  Round of Sixteen – Argentina : Mexico (2:1 – OT)

- 11 p.m. to 12 a.m., Fan Garden
  Rhythm & Brass Band – The best of rock, pop, soul & funk

- 11 p.m. to 12 a.m., Stiftsplatz
  K-Town Allstars – feat. Stephan Flesch – the finest soul and pop

■ ■ ■

Cie. Midi 12 in action.

Sunday, 25 June

Because of the enthusiastic response to the matches of the German national team, the World Cup Office checks on an additional location for a giant screen. It shall be in Barbarossastraße. Italian state TV Rai reports live from Martinsplatz despite the rain. However, the program at the two Public Viewing locations must be temporarily interrupted due to a thunderstorm and high winds.
What a pity: The Japanese band Gocoo has to pack up its drums.

90°F
32°C

Lulu Weiss Ensemble

"Without Holland, we will go ..."

Events on this day

- Street Theater Festival, World Cup Mile
  Cia. Sarruga, Cie. Midi 12, Cie. Albédo, Theater Pikante
- approx. 1 to 2.45 p.m., Stiftsplatz
  Saarbruck Libre – Six full-blood musicians singing in the Saarbrücken dialect
- 1 to 3 p.m., Fan Garden
  Kolpingblasorchester Kaiserslautern 1912 e.V. – Concert music and popular music
- 1 to 4 p.m., World Cup Mile
  Esprit, KL WM Jam Band – Marching bands
- 1 to 5 p.m., downtown
  Lulu Weiss Ensemble – Marching band
- approx. 3 to 4.15 p.m., Stiftsplatz
  Special Request Band – Reggae, soca and calypso
- 4 to 5 p.m., Fan Garden
  Campfire Kings – The band with its own campfire
- ⚽ 5 p.m., FAN FEST Public Viewing
  Round of Sixteen – England : Ecuador (1:0)
- 7 to 9 p.m., World Cup Mile
  Esprit, Jack's Blues Caravane – Marching bands
- 7 to 9 p.m., Fan Garden
  Campfire Kings – The band with its own campfire
- ⚽ 9 p.m., FAN FEST Public Viewing
  Round of Sixteen – Portugal : Netherlands (1:0)
- 11 p.m. to 1 a.m., Stiftsplatz
  Gocoo – Japanese Taiko (drum) group
- 11 p.m. to 12 a.m., Fan Garden
  Campfire Kings – The band with its own campfire
- ■ ■ ■

Monday, 26 June

The city doubles its population: More than 100,000 guests are in the city. After the match: Sad Australians, happy Italians. Still, both celebrate. The final whistle is blown on the World Cup matches in Kaiserslautern. But: The Caribbean returns: The rapso kings of "Brothers Resistance" are visiting, chasing away the last remnants of dark clouds. For the students of the city, normality also returns. On match days, the schools had remained closed, also because the buses were needed for the World Cup visitors.

And this is what the sticker looked like when it was printed. (continued from 22 June)

25°C
77°F

Welcome back, Italy and Australia!

Australian lovers' talk

Cheers!

Fans in contest.

Mein Spieltipp:

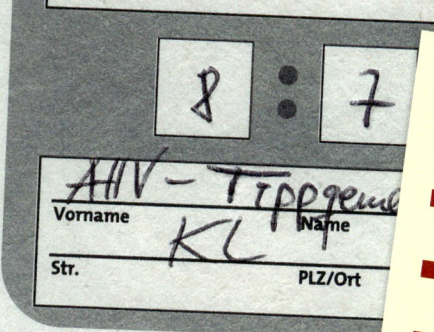

Italien gegen Australien

8 : 7

Vorname: AHV-Tippgeme...
Name: ...
Str.: KL
PLZ/Ort:

Good bye, Australia. Football can sometimes be cruel. You have changed Kaiserslautern, you have delighted us with your joie de vivre and your cordiality. See you. Hopefully soon.

Events on this day

- Street Theater Festival, World Cup Mile
  Cie. Midi 12, Cie. Albédo
- 1 to 3.30 p.m., Fan Garden
  King Tchisa – Independent Pop-Rock unplugged
- 1 to 4 p.m., World Cup Mile
  KL WM Jam Band, Phönix Jazzband – Marching bands
- approx. 1 to 4.15 p.m., Stiftsplatz
  Ethnova Orkestra – HeartPeopleWorldMusic
- 1 to 5 p.m., Schillerplatz
  Der Hausfreund – Marching band
- 4 to 5 p.m., Fan Garden
  Ringo Ska – Beatles songs in Ska- and reggae sound
- ⚽ 5 p.m., FAN FEST Public Viewing, Stadion
  Round of Sixteen – Italy : Australia (1:0)
- approx. 7 to 7.20 p.m., Stiftsplatz
  Brothers Resistance – King of Rapso from Trinidad & Tobago
- 7 to 9 p.m., World Cup Mile
  KL WM Jam Band, Blaskreis Grün Weiß – Marching bands
- 7 to 9 p.m., Fan Garden
  Ringo Ska – Beatles songs in Ska- and reggae sound
- ⚽ 9 p.m., FAN FEST Public Viewing
  Round of Sixteen – Switzerland : Ukraine (0:3 – after penalty shoot out)
- 11 p.m. to 1 a.m., Fan Garden
  Ringo Ska – Beatles-Songs im Ska- und Reggae-Sound
- 11 p.m. to 1 a.m., Stiftsplatz
  Brothers Resistance – King of Rapso from Trinidad & Tobago
- ■ ■ ■

Tuesday, 27 June

The World Cup Mile is open for the last time. This event mile has become known all over Germany. Now it is over. The Lord Mayor takes stock – and draws his hat before his citizens: "Thank you, Kaiserslautern!" And: The party continues anyway.

81°F 27°C

Vielen Dank KAISERSLAUTERN!

Vielen Dank an über 1.000.000 Gäste aus aller Welt, an alle Anwohner und Bürger, an alle Sponsoren und Partner, an alle Dienstleister, Künstler, Volunteers und Helfer.

Bernhard J. Deubig
Oberbürgermeister der Stadt Kaiserslautern

Erwin Saile
WM-Koordinator der Stadt Kaiserslautern

FIFA WM-STADT
KL KAISERSLAUTERN

Football is a sport for everyone.

Companie d'Outre Rue on 23 June

Great entertainment.

Still Collins

Events on this day

- 1 to 3 p.m., Fan Garden
  Stadtkapelle Pirmasens – Brass music and more
- 1 to 4 p.m., World Cup Mile
  Jack's Blues Caravane, KL WM Jam Band – Marching bands
- approx. 1 to 4.15 p.m., Stiftsplatz
  K-Town WM-Band – Great sound from pop to rock
- 4 to 5 p.m., Fan Garden
  French Touch – Tango and musette
- 5 p.m., FAN FEST Public Viewing
  Round of Sixteen – Brazil : Ghana (3:0)
- approx. 7 to 7.20 p.m., Stiftsplatz
  K-Town WM-Band – Great sound from pop to rock
- 7 to 9 p.m., World Cup Mile
  Jack's Blues Caravane, H. Krüger & Low Budget – Marching bands
- 7 to 9 p.m., Fan Garden
  Still Collins – Europe's Phil Collins & Genesis Tribute Band No. 1
- 9 p.m., FAN FEST Public Viewing
  Round of Sixteen – Spain : France (1:3)
- 11 p.m. – 12 a.m., Stiftsplatz
  K-Town WM-Band – Great sound from pop to rock
- 11 p.m. – 12 a.m., Fan Garden
  Still Collins – Europe's Phil Collins & Genesis Tribute Band No. 1
- ...

Wednesday, 28 June

No match today. "Bleifrei" is playing. And there is a cult night. The 70s and 80s. Does anybody want to listen to this? Yes. Memory is the only paradise that nobody can evict us from.

77°F / 25°C

Events on this day

- 4 to 7 p.m., Stiftsplatz
  Bleifrei – 'Lead-free' – Blowing the lead out of its listeners' bones
- 8 p.m. to 12 a.m., Stiftsplatz
  The 1st Kaiserslautern 70s & 80s Cult Night – with DJ Bob Murawka & the "Zeitreise (Time Travel)" of Snailshouse

Bleifrei

Snailshouse

The last performance of "Salto Culinare"

Kaiserslautern even has its own World Cup cup!

Thursday, 29 June

The preparations for the quarterfinals are going on. In Kaiserslautern, too. Chart breaker Revolverheld turns up the heat on Stiftsplatz.

79°F 26°C

Events on this day

- 1 to 3 p.m., Stiftsplatz
  Landespolizeiorchester Rheinland-Pfalz – Swinging into the summer
- 5 to 6 p.m., Stiftsplatz
  running five – Rock 'n' roll from Jerry Lee Lewis to Elvis Presley
- 6 to 7.30 p.m., Stiftsplatz
  Midnight Movers – Playing the classics of soul
- 8 to 9.30 p.m., Stiftsplatz
  K 4711 – Four women provide first aid in rock
- 10 p.m. to 12 a.m., Stiftsplatz
  Revolverheld

Midnight Movers

Revolverheld

I got it!
One of the commemorative coins minted on the occasion of the World Cup!

Friday, 30 June

81°F
27°C

15,000 fans watch the victory of "Klinsmann's Boys" against Argentina. The report of the police and the emergency services is very short: Nothing special happened. Great!

Events on this day

- approx. 1 to 2.45 p.m., Stiftsplatz
  X-pression – Let's have a party!!
- approx. 3 to 4.15 p.m., Stiftsplatz
  K-Town WM-Band – Great sound from pop to rock
- ⚽ 5 p.m., FAN FEST Public Viewing
  Quarterfinals – Germany : Argentina (5:3 – after penalty shoot-out)
- approx. 7 to 7.20 p.m., Stiftsplatz
  K-Town WM-Band – Great sound from pop to rock
- 7 to 9 p.m., Schillerplatz
  Skiffle Tigers – Marching band
- ⚽ 9 p.m., FAN FEST Public Viewing
  Quarterfinals – Italy : Ukraine (3:0)
- 11 p.m. to 1 a.m., Stiftsplatz
  The Gypsys – Multicultural party rock

Nothing special happened...

Germany is celebrating because...

... we made it into the semi-finals!

Saturday, 1 July

Portugal kicks England out of the race, France kicks out Brazil. The Portuguese population in Kaiserslautern is overjoyed.

82°F ☀ 28°C

Events on this day

- approx. 1 to 2.45 p.m., Stiftsplatz
  Rock Heroes – 20 years of rock history
- approx. 3 to 4.15 p.m., Stiftsplatz
  All that – The finest in Black Music
- ⚽ 5 p.m., FAN FEST Public Viewing
  Quarterfinals – England : Portugal (1:3 – after penalty shoot-out)
- approx. 7 to 7.20 p.m., Stiftsplatz
  All that – The finest in Black Music
- 7 to 9 p.m., Schillerplatz
  Red Hot Dixie Devils – Marching band
- ⚽ 9 p.m., FAN FEST Public Viewing
  Quarterfinals – Brazil : France (0:1)
- 11 p.m. to 1 a.m., Stiftsplatz
  K-Town Allstars – feat. Stephan Flesch – The finest of soul & pop
- ...

England and Portugal understood each other well.

84°F / 29°C

Sunday, 2 July

When football takes a break, it's music's turn: Swing with Roger Cicero on the Stiftsplatz stage. And a living legend of jazz: Klaus Doldinger. "Tatort Kaiserslautern" ('Crime Scene Kaiserslautern'). In the Fruchthalle, the topic is also good and bad luck – just like in football: The soundscapes of the opera Carmina Burana intoxicate the audience.

Events on this day

- 3 to 5 p.m., Stiftsplatz
  KL WM Jam Band – The special jazz experience
- 3 to 5 p.m., Altenhof
  Kolpingkapelle Kindsbach – The works of H. L. Blankenburg
- 5 p.m., Fruchthalle
  Carmina Burana Monumental Opera – Intoxicating soundscapes combine classical and pop music
- 6 to 8 p.m., Stiftsplatz
  Roger Cicero – New German Swing
- 8 p.m., Pfalztheater
  Rock Opera Abydos – The sensational success by Andy Kuntz
- 8.30 p.m., Kammgarn
  Theatersport WM – The USA improvising against Slovenia
- 9 to 11 p.m., Stiftsplatz
  Klaus Doldinger's Passport – "Tatort Kaiserslautern" ('Crime Scene Kaiserslautern')

"Tatort Kaiserslautern" ('Crime Scene Kaiserslautern')

Monday, 3 July

Researchers of the University of Kaiserslautern present the world's smallest football field. It is half a micrometer in length, corresponding to a scale of 1:210 million. One could put about 20,000 of these football fields on a single hair. Physicist Dr. Stefan Trellenkamp developed this to answer a call to German science issued by "Spiegel online".

86°F
30°C

Events on this day

- 3 to 7 p.m., Stiftsplatz
  Exxes – The finest cover rock/pop
- 7.30 to 9.30 p.m., Stiftsplatz
  Boppin'B – Twenty Years of Rockin' Tour
- 10 p.m. to 12 a.m., Stiftsplatz
  The BossHoss – Germany's most successful country-rock band

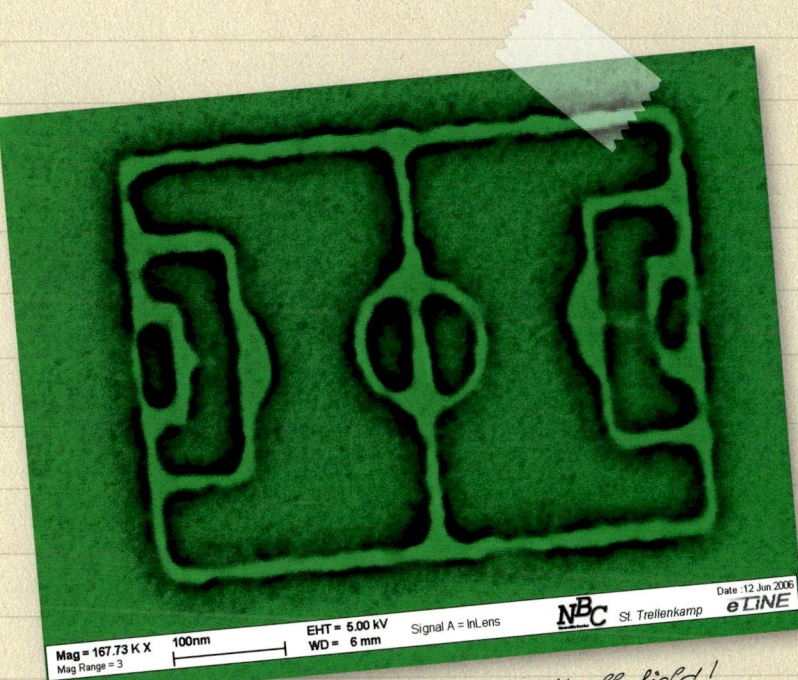

If you find us, you'll like us!

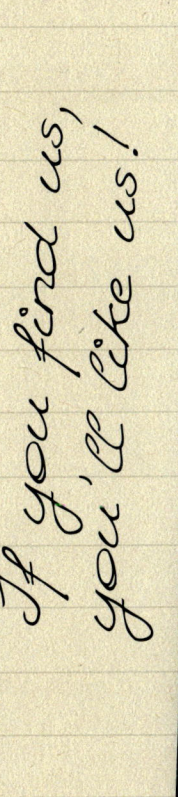

The world's smallest football field!

Tuesday, 4 July

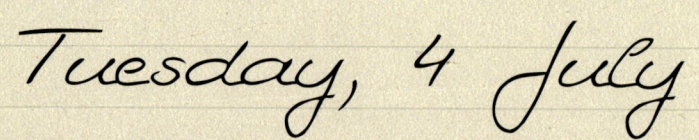

An ocean of flags in black, red, and gold. 15,000 fans are cheering on the German team in the semi-final match against Italy – in vain. For one evening, nobody feels like eating pizza!

90°F ☀ 32°C

Events on this day

- approx. 1 to 4.45 p.m., Stiftsplatz
  K-Town WM-Band – Great sound from pop to rock
- approx. 4.45 to 5.45 p.m., Stiftsplatz
  Tommy the Clown – With the hip hop clowns – Rize live
- approx. 6.30 to 7.15 p.m., Stiftsplatz
  Mr. Williams – #1 Robbie Williams Cover Show
- 7 to 9 p.m., Schillerplatz
  H. Krüger & Low Budget – Marching band
- ⚽ 9 p.m., FAN FEST Public Viewing
  Semi-Finals – Germany : Italy (0:2 – OT)
- 11 p.m. – 1 a.m., Stiftsplatz
  Mr. Williams – #1 Robbie Williams Cover Show

■ ■ ■

Game over...

Italy is cheering...

... and honking triumphantly.

Mr. Williams

Wednesday, 5 July

Between the sounds of Stephan Flesch and the K-Town All Stars, the second team to play in the finals is determined: France wins over Portugal. Many women are saying that it won't be so bad if we don't win the World Cup. Then we would just do it next year…

88°F 31°C

Events on this day

- approx. 1 to 4 p.m., Stiftsplatz
  "the new generation" Classic&Pop – The top-class show orchestra
- approx. 4.45 to 7.15 p.m., Stiftsplatz
  K-Town Allstars – feat. Stephan Flesch – The finest of soul & pop
- 7 to 9 p.m., Schillerplatz
  La Zizique Chanson Band – Marching band
- ⚽ 9 p.m., FAN FEST Public Viewing
  Semi-Finals – Portugal : France (0:1)
- 11 p.m. to 12 a.m., Stiftsplatz
  K-Town Allstars – feat. Stephan Flesch – The finest of soul & pop

"The voice" Stephan Flesch

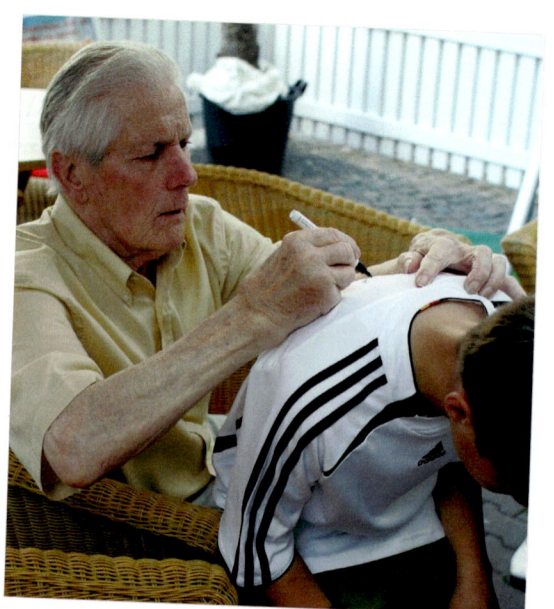

Autographs by Ottmar Walter are still popular

Cheers! The World Cup Wine

Thursday, 6 July

The "Swiss Robbie Williams" arrives wearing a baseball cap and shorts. Patrick Nuo has many female fans. But he cannot compete with the stars of the Queen musical "We Will Rock You": "The show must go on!" Just a few days to go...

81°F
27°C

Events on this day

- 3 to 6 p.m., Stiftsplatz
  Greencard – Bold and rocking
- 7 to 9 p.m., Stiftsplatz
  Patrick Nuo
- 10 p.m. to 12 a.m., Stiftsplatz
  We Rock – The original band from the Cologne Queen musical "We Will Rock You"

Patrick Nuo

Friday, 7 July

The Old Town Festival is opened. A new World Cup Mile? From Martinsplatz to Mainzer Tor, people are having fun. Eight additional stages start to compete with the Stiftsplatz.

26°C
79°F

Archers at the Medieval Market

Music group "All That"

Events on this day

- 5 to 7 p.m., Stiftsplatz
  FABO – Farbian Harloff
- 7 to 1 p.m., Old Town
  Old Town Festival – The festival mile from St. Martinsplatz to Mainzer Tor
- 8 to 9 p.m., Stiftsplatz
  DRai – Catchy rock melodies with meaningful texts
- 10 to 11 p.m., Stiftsplatz
  Noah Eps – Songwriting made in Germany
- 11 p.m. to 1 a.m., Stiftsplatz
  Groovin' Affairs – Funk, Soul, Pop, Rock at its best
- ■ ■ ■

Saturday, 8 July

A mixture of city festival and the great world of football. 20,000 visitors come to the Old Town Festival, 10,000 celebrated the German team's third place on the public viewing screens. And Christina Baralt from Steinalben becomes the new Miss Kaiserslautern.

81°F 27°C

Old Town meets World Cup

Smile, please...

K-Town WM-Band

Events on this day

- 11 to 1 a.m., Old Town
  Old Town Festival – The festival mile from St. Martinsplatz to Mainzer Tor
- approx. 1 to 4 p.m., Stiftsplatz
  NIK Miller and the groovin' tunes – Soul & pop
- approx. 4.30 to 7.15 p.m., Stiftsplatz
  Jomtones – Rock 'n' reggae
- ⚽ 9 p.m., FAN FEST Public Viewing
  Match for third place – Germany : Portugal (3:1)
- 11 p.m. to 1 a.m., Stiftsplatz
  K-Town WM-Band – Great sound from pop to rock

■ ■ ■

The "little" finals

Even a third place is received enthusiastically.

Sunday, 9 July

Italian night in Kaiserslautern. The tifosi celebrate their fourth World Cup title. Motorcade. "Azzuro" is chanted from hoarse throats. Even the Germans enjoy their pizza again. And it is even free today. Match over.

84°F
29°C

When France was still full of hope

And not anymore...

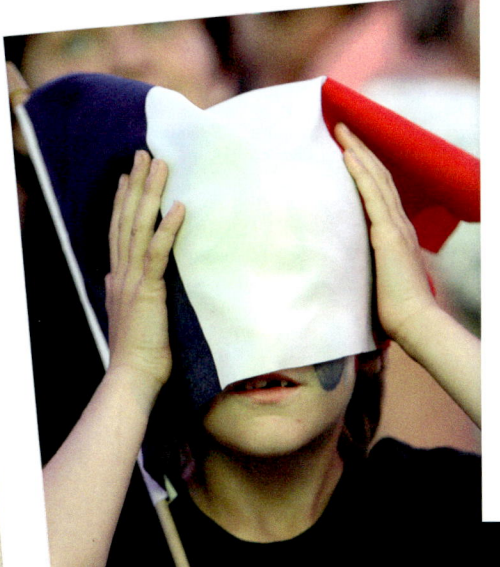

I can't stand looking at them anymore...

... at these cheering Italians.

How did an Italian journalist put it so nicely: "The Pope is German, but God is Italian."

Events on this day

- **11 to 1 a.m., Old Town**
  Old Town Festival – The festival mile from St. Martinsplatz to Mainzer Tor
- **approx. 1 to 2.30 p.m., Stiftsplatz**
  Sweat – Funk, soul and black music
- **approx. 3.30 – 4.30 p.m., Stiftsplatz**
  Guerilla Bar – German pop with Latin influences
- **4 to 8 p.m., Schillerplatz**
  KL WM Jam Band – Marching band
- **approx. 5.15 to 6 p.m., Stiftsplatz**
  Thaibnakkel – Hip rockers from Mainz with unusual sounds
- ⚽ **8 to 9.45 p.m., FAN FEST Public Viewing**
  Final – Italy : France (6:4 – after penalty shoot-out)
- **10.30 to 10.45 p.m., Stiftsplatz**
  Final Fireworks – The great goodbye
- **10.30 p.m. to 1 a.m., Stiftsplatz**
  LIVIN' music family – The sound of dance & soul

Emotions...

QUOTE ...

"I HAVE NEVER BEFORE seen a soccer World Cup associated with such a large festival. I think that this is the World Cup of the people."

Jorge Valdano, Argentinean ex-world champion

ROLLER-COASTER OF EMOTIONS: *During the World Cup, nobody remained unaffected. From overwhelming euphoria to total desperation, the fans lived through all the heights and depths with their teams.*

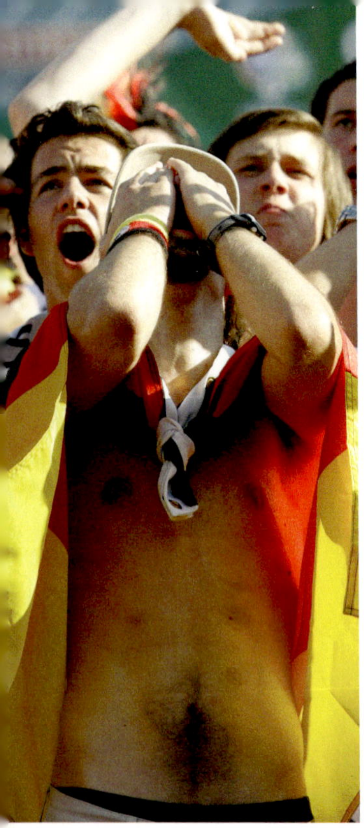
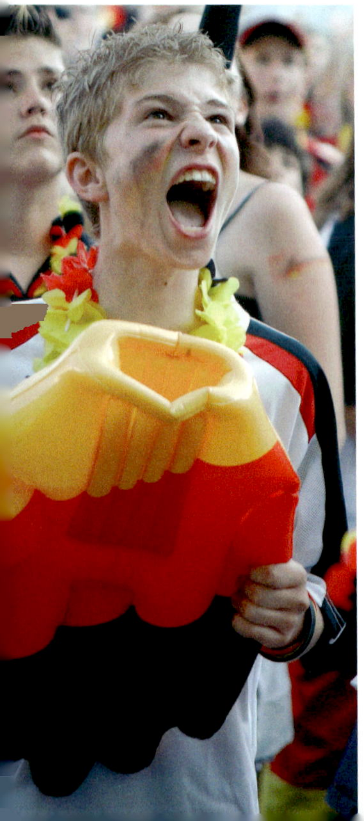
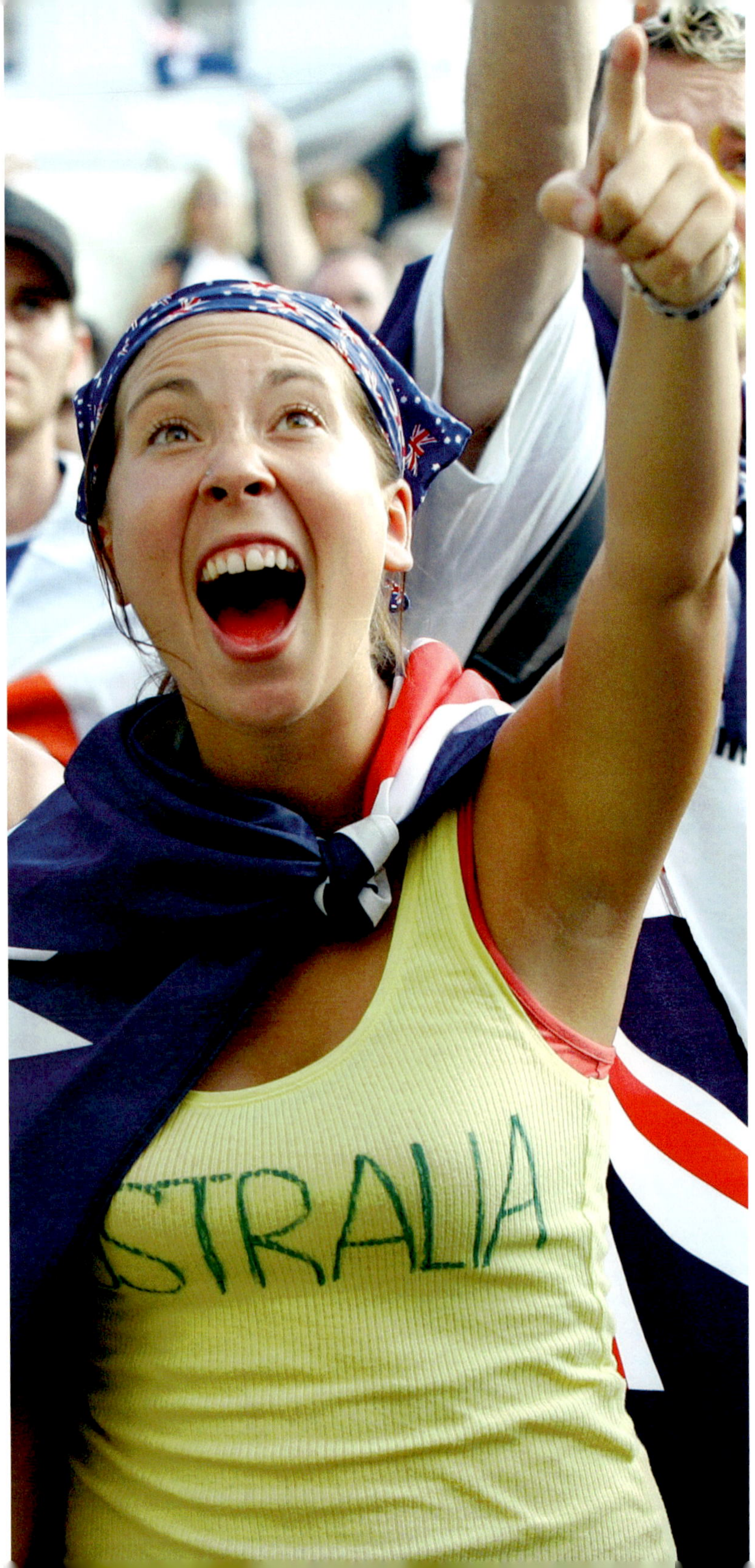
STRALIA
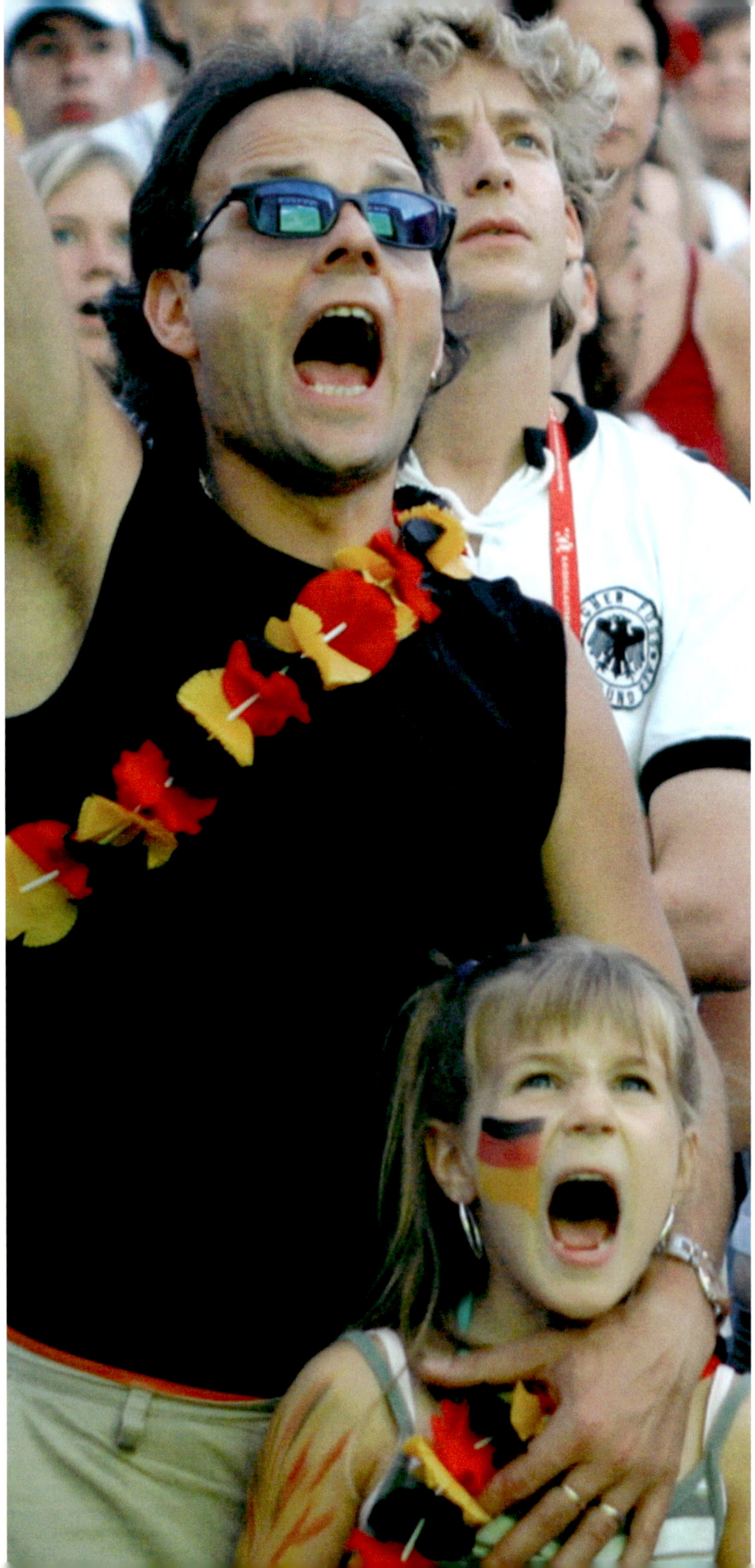
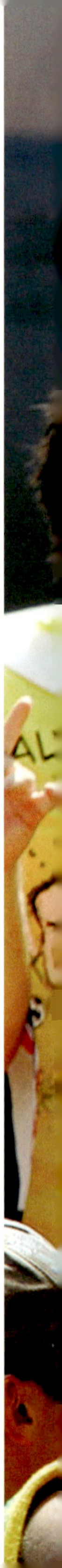

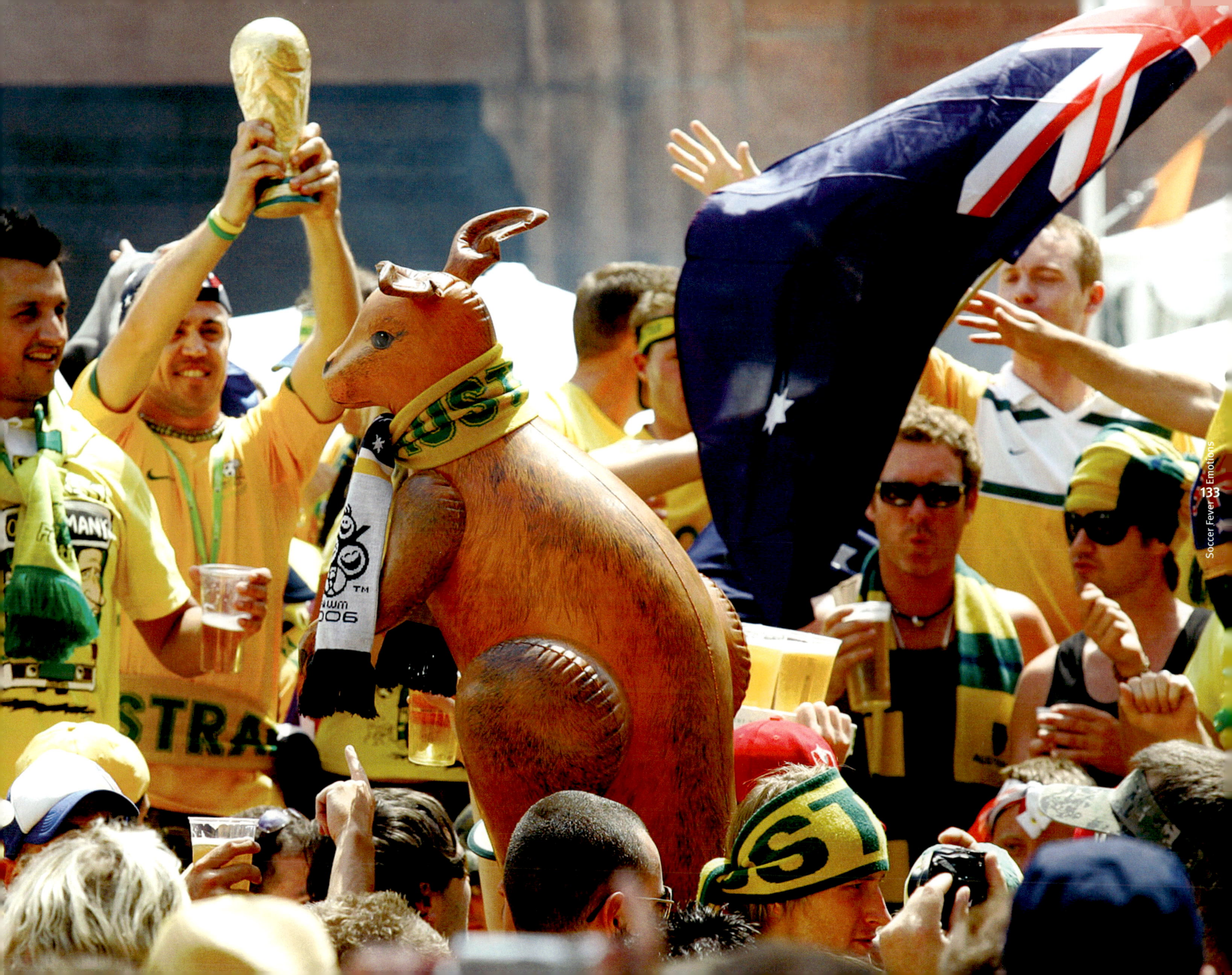

Soccer Fever Emotions

134

VOICES ...

"IN THE OLD TOWN AREA of Kaiserslautern, the Americans are assembling, Americans who are not soldiers or marines, with their wives and children. In the afternoon sun, Stars and Stripes in a blue ocean – the Italians have already conquered the center of Kaiserslautern. Italians from Italy and from Germany together in their hearts, not only in the stadium. A pedestrian island in the costume of the world champion, in the name of beer. The guys in royal blue and the beer marry on the market square. The fan fest becomes frenetic."

La Gazzetta Sportiva, Italy

136 Soccer Fever Emotions

Sure, the German fans waved their flags, black-red-gold wristbands and necklaces were in, as was the collective fan flag on the cars. Together they all sang the national anthem, as though this was the most natural thing to do. Again and again. Without any bad conscience. The 2006 FIFA World Cup has developed a new national feeling. Without any pathos and Germanomania. Not tense, almost fresh, but never suspicious. In the summer of 2006, the Germans also learned a new way of dealing with their national symbols. A more normal way.

138 Soccer Fever Emotions

139

FINALS: Italy wins against France and becomes the world champion. The numerous Italian fans are overjoyed and celebrate all night.

Emotions

Even philosophers have pondered victory and defeat in sports. Soccer history knows grandiose triumphs, historical successes, but also traumatic defeats. Regarding this issue, the 2006 FIFA World Cup will certainly not leave very deep traces. Of course, the World Cup success of the Italians was not something to be expected necessarily, considering the manipulation scandal in their own country, but it certainly was no sensation. Even the victory of Australia over Japan was not a real surprise, but still, it will occupy a place in the sports history books of the fifth continent: It was the first victory at any World Cup, ever. Results are more than mere numbers, more than statistical accessories of a great party. For a few hours, they put people into the most diverse moods. Hardly anyone can escape the radiant power of victory and defeat. People are touched, moved to the core, become ecstatic, or fall into deep depressions. Usually only for a few hours. But still. In soccer, even men may cry.

QUOTE ...

"EVEN IF GERMANY was not in the finals, it won, because it hosted the best World Cup of all times and united the nation in this effort."

*Kofi Annan,
UN Secretary General*

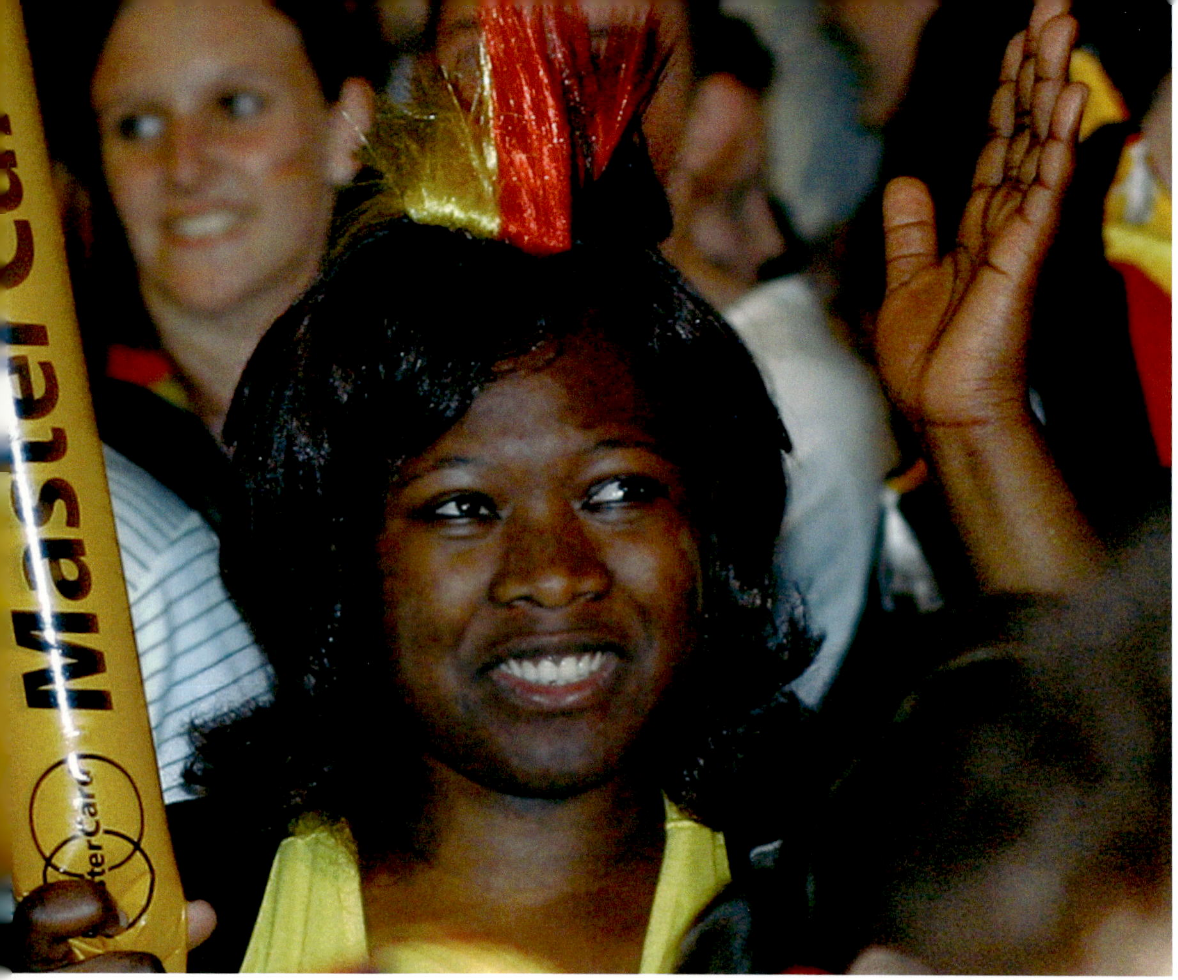

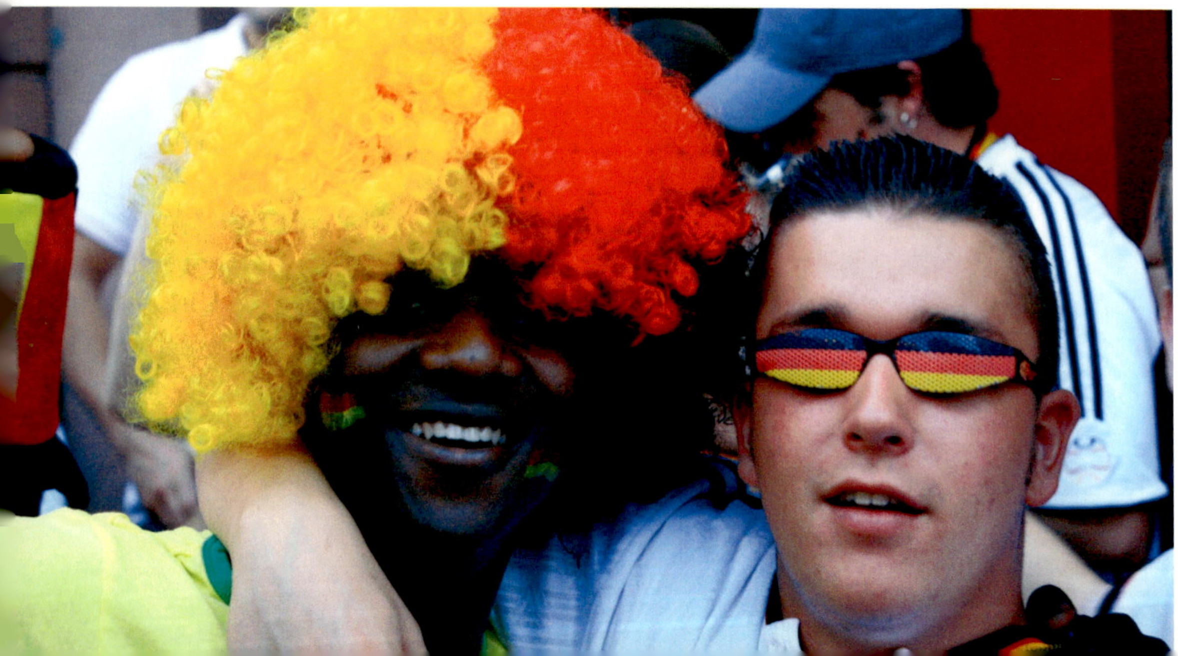

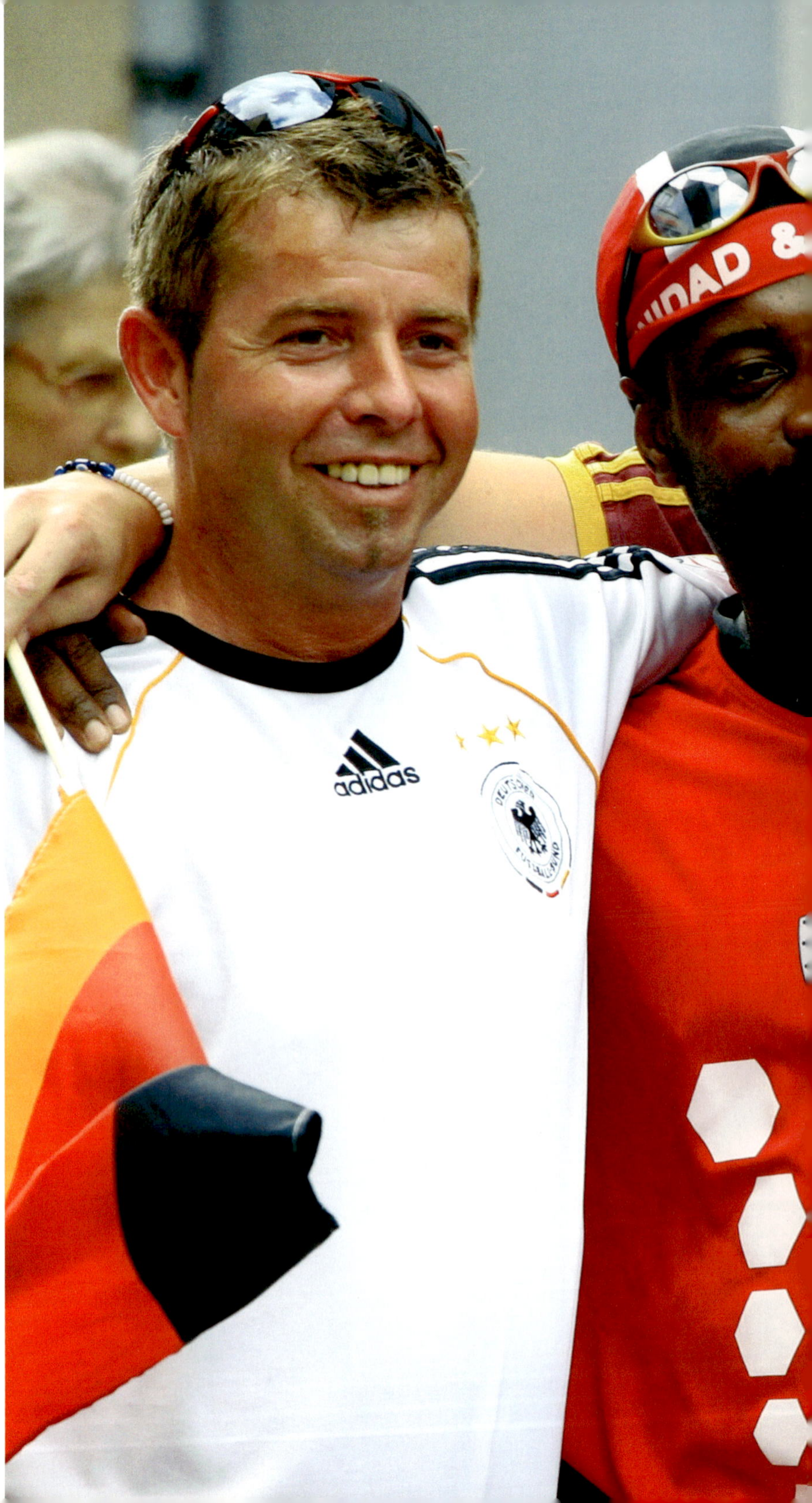
adidas

A time to make friends

A time
to make friends

Maybe Kaiserslautern was just lucky as far as the drawing was concerned. Nevertheless, part of the credit also goes to the organizers for making sure that the wonderful guests actually did feel well in Kaiserslautern. Peacefully, happily, and exuberantly, about one million people celebrated their own personal World Cup for 31 days. Up to 120,000 guests a day presented a logistical challenge to the city. And nothing happened ...

MOMENTS ...

TWO DANISH soccer fans who wanted to watch the World Cup match Spain against Saudi-Arabia asked a family for directions to the campground – and were immediately invited to spend the night free of charge. "They did not want any money", raved 28-year-old Henrik.

Benvenuto! ¡Bienvenidos! Welcome! أهلاً وسهلاً ¡Bienvenidos!

Australia   Italy   Japan   Paraguay

A time
to make friends

... or did it? The people in the city seemed to have literally absorbed the motto of the World Cup. Some celebrated hand in hand with the international guests, others stood on the side, marveling, until they, too, got infected by this easygoingness. Scenes took place that appeared unreal. The picture of Australians celebrating in front of the illuminated Stiftskirche church, carrying kangaroos on their backs, dancing to the sounds of the 1980s classical hit "Down under" by the band "Men at work", has burned itself into the minds of many Kaiserslautern citizens. Into their memories. And into their hearts. Don't let anybody say that the World Cup had no long-term effects ...

Saudi-Arabia **Spain** **Trinidad and Tobago** **USA**

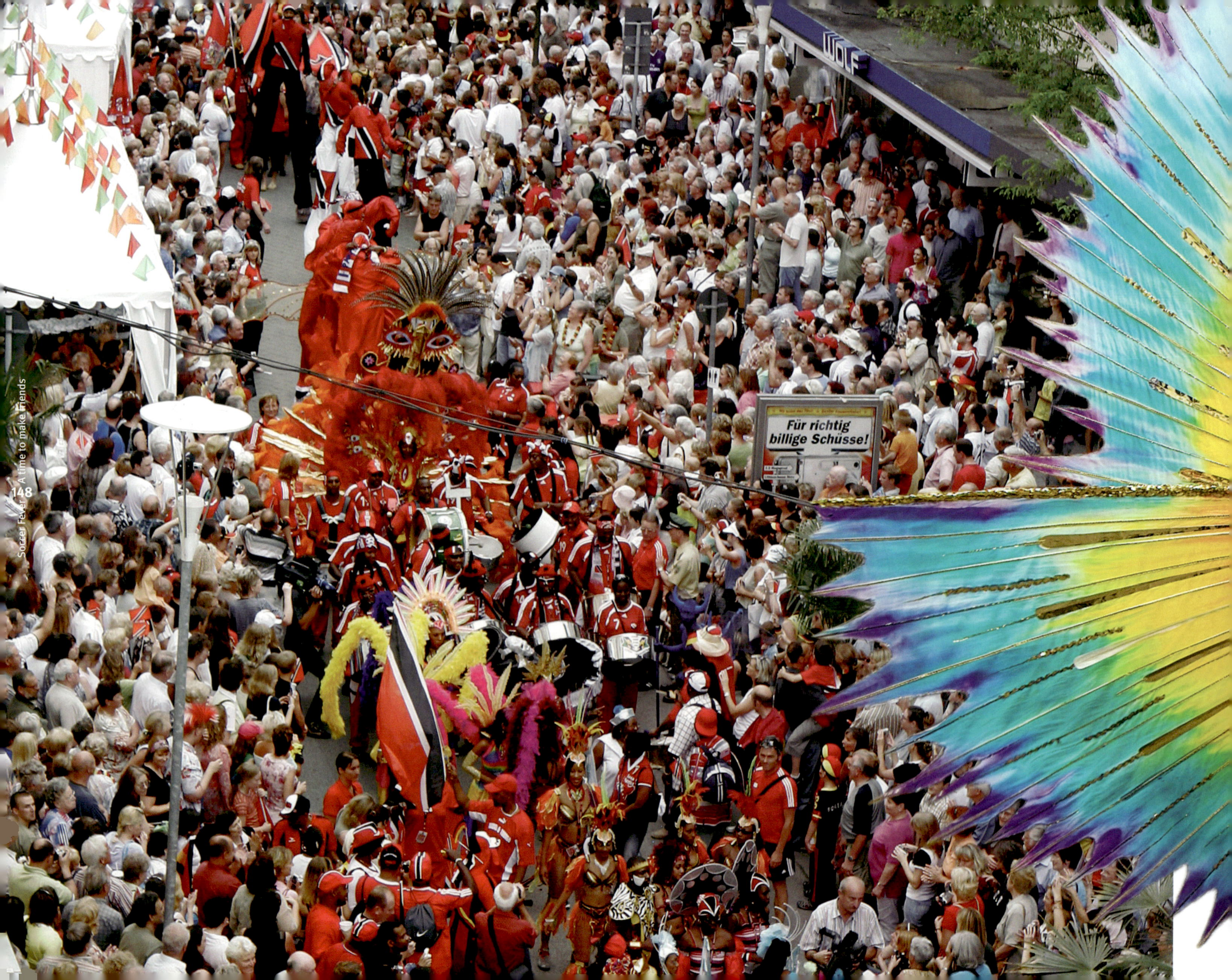
WOLF
Für richtig
billige Schüsse!

FASCINATING: **The beauty of the Caribbean**

MOMENTS …

THANKS TO some helpful employees of the city of Kaiserslautern, two soccer fans from Trinidad and Tobago were able to get on their return flight to the Caribbean, even though they had lost their passports the night before. Without passports, they would have had to cancel the flight, which would have caused enormous costs for the two unlucky persons. Three city employees got in touch with a colleague in the stadium via the World Cup Office – and this colleague reported the problem directly to the ambassador. She, in turn, immediately called the embassy of the Caribbean nation in London, which transferred documents to the airport. Only passport photos were still missing – and since these were not that easy to get anymore late at night, the police jumped in and took pictures of the two fans. At one thirty in the morning, an employee of the municipal public order office received a phone call from the airport – everything had worked out, the two soccer fans were able to get on their flight back home and were very thankful for the effort invested by the authorities in Kaiserslautern. "A time to make friends" – this is exactly how it felt in the smallest World Cup host city, they said.

The whole city is World Cup …

If you saw the numerous signs and flags, you must have gotten the impression that "World Cup outposts" were distributed across the whole city. And somehow this was true. Whereas the FIFA Organizing Committee had its ticket volunteer center in Kohlenhofstraße, the city's World Cup Office occupied various locations: The volunteers met in the old town, the artists and security personnel at Stiftsplatz, and the emergency medical personnel at Eselsfürth.

Together with the state, with Lotto Rheinland-Pfalz, with Stadtsparkasse and Südwestrundfunk, the city had established a VIP area in the Stiftskeller; only a stone's throw away was the Media Point, the joint press center of the city and the police, point of contact for national and international journalists. Actually, you could feel the World Cup everywhere. And see it. Of course, functionality was not neglected, either: The Tourist Information Office, where guests often made their first contacts, not only made hotel reservations, but also gave away paper flags to the soccer fans.

At "Kniebrech", three associations made their areas available for a fan camp. More than 6,000 guests made use of it. The motor home parking lots on the Daenner Parking Lot, in Dansenberg, and in Hohenecken were much frequented.

Tor zum Betzenberg

Willkommen bei Freunden
Fritz-Walter Stammtisch

VOICES ...

"KAISERSLAUTERN became a stroke of luck for the World Cup in Germany. The spirit behind the World Cup, namely friendship among peoples, became experienceable in a special way in this Western Palatinate city. ... The people of Kaiserslautern proved during the past days of the World Cup that they are open and capable of enthusiasm; they let themselves be carried away by the internationality, the exuberance, and the colorfulness. The city demonstrated that it is efficient and capable; its preparation for the World Cup was excellent. ... The city of Kaiserslautern has made good use of the chances offered by the World Cup. With its World Cup performance, it brought honor to the Palatinate and to Rheinland-Pfalz ... It was right for Kaiserslautern and the state to make the decision to host the World Cup. Today, this enthusiasm finally proves them right!"

Die Rheinpfalz, Germany

The whole city is World Cup

VOICES ...

"KAISERSLAUTERN is a workers' city, not far from the border with Luxembourg, and as in most of the cities, the dominating food are sausages. Bratwurst ('grilled sausage'). Rindswurst ('grilled beef sausage'). Whatever-kind of sausage. I am no expert in this field, but they got me: I think they have the best sausages in Kaiserslautern ... Maybe all of Kaiserslautern conspired to be on its best behavior during the World Cup, but in those three days that I spent here, I only heard one car honk, for example, and that was when Germany won against Poland. Ask someone for directions – even while he is driving – you will get help. Often, the people even accompanied me part of the way. As in many German cities, most people here speak English and were happy to practice it on me: 'Are you from California?' 'No, Florida.' 'Ah, Florida. The alligators are dangerous, yes?' 'Yes', I reply. 'Just don't go swimming with them.' " ...

West Palm Beach, USA

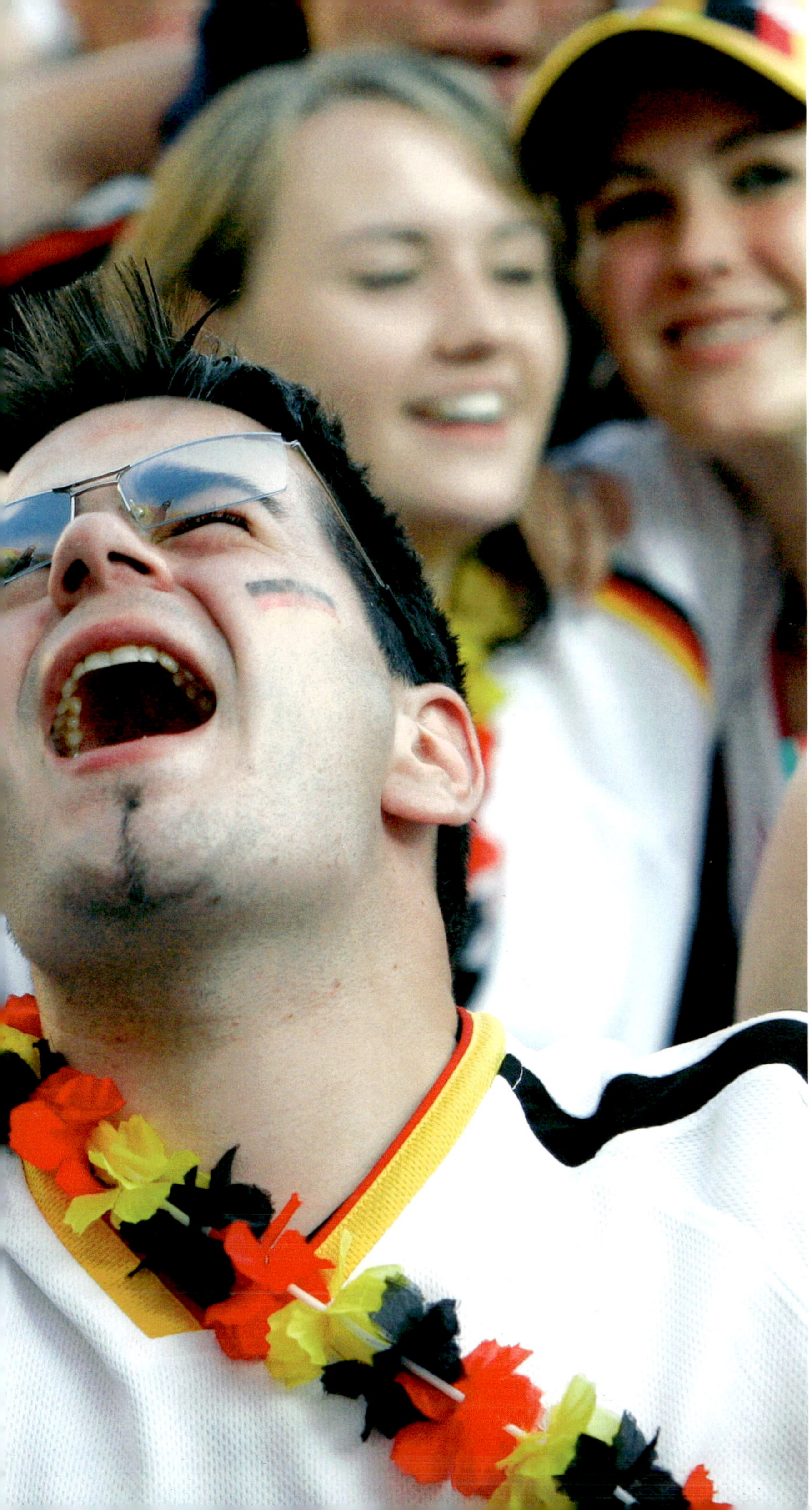

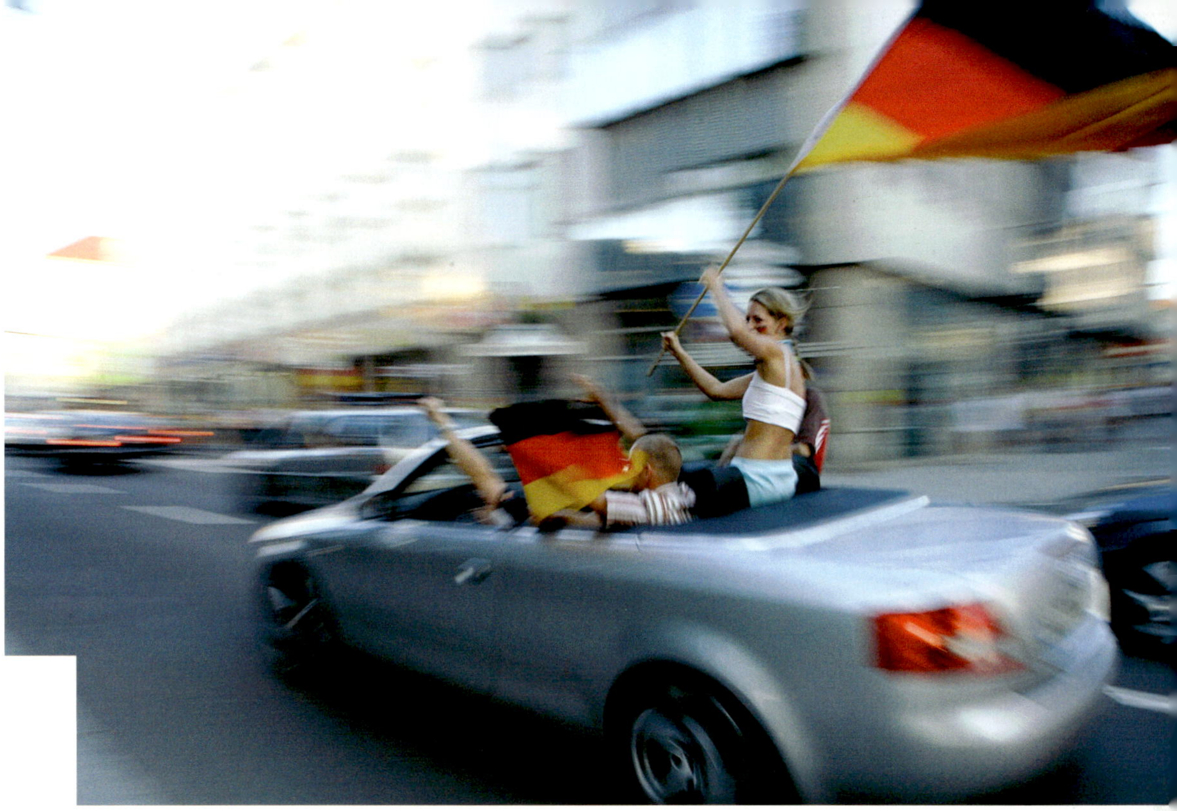

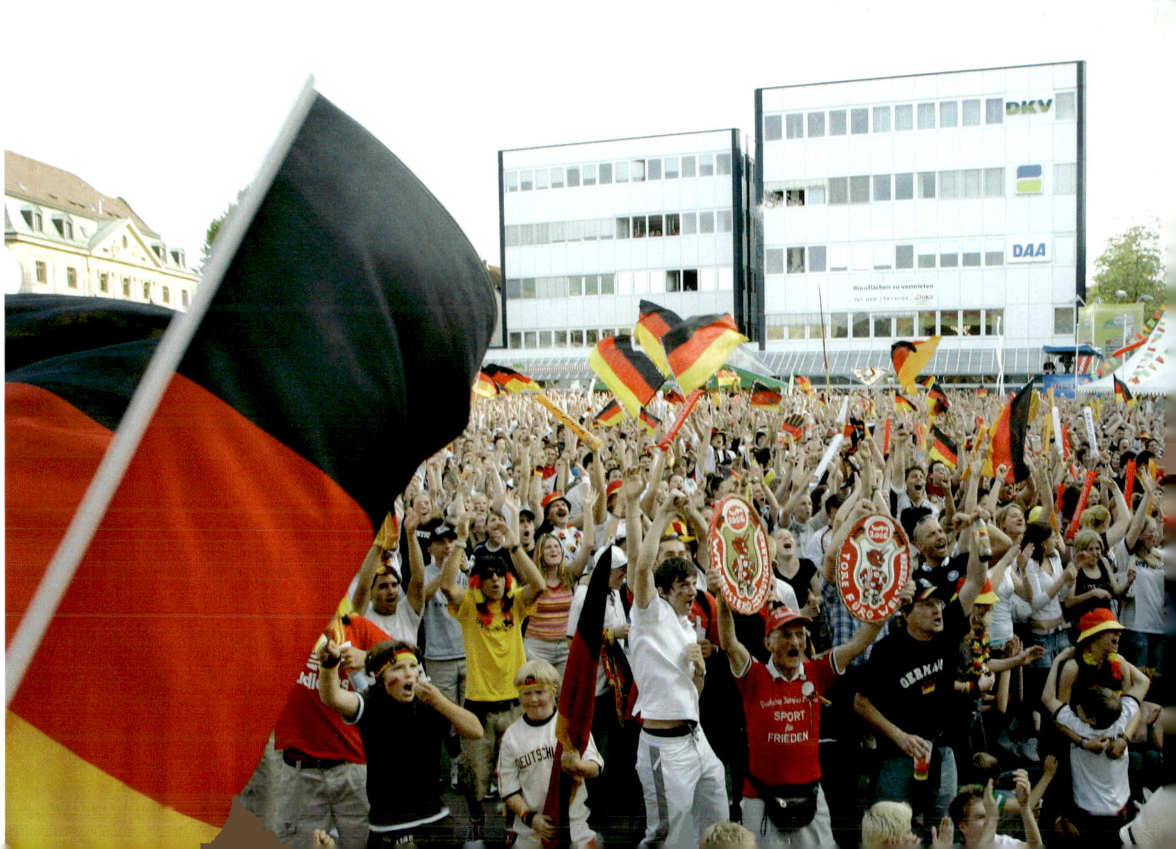
DKV
DAA
SPORT
FRIEDEN

WM 2006

Herz
Benve
Bier

All "dressed up"

The city got its Sunday suit out of the wardrobe for the World Cup. And dressed up. Numerous green spaces were carefully designed with the World Cup in mind. At Schillerplatz and in Donnersbergstraße, the incoming fans were greeted with over-dimensional "Welcome" signs in the respective national languages; hundreds of flags were flying all over town.

QUOTE ...

"HATS OFF TO YOU, Kaiserslautern, worthy of a world champion! Kaiserslautern and the Palatinate have shown themselves to be grandiose hosts."

Dr. Markus Merk,
World Cup Referee

The "11 Friends" inside the Löwenburgkreisel traffic circle have long ago become a popular and prominent element in the Kaiserslautern cityscape. A few days before the start of the World Cup, this work of art was complemented by sculptures of eight players dressed in the shirts of the nations hosted by Kaiserslautern, which were set up on Philipp-Mees-Platz, as well as by three soccer fans sitting on the wall at the traffic circle. Shortly before the match of the round of sixteen, two more players with the shirts of the Italian and the Australian national teams were set up.

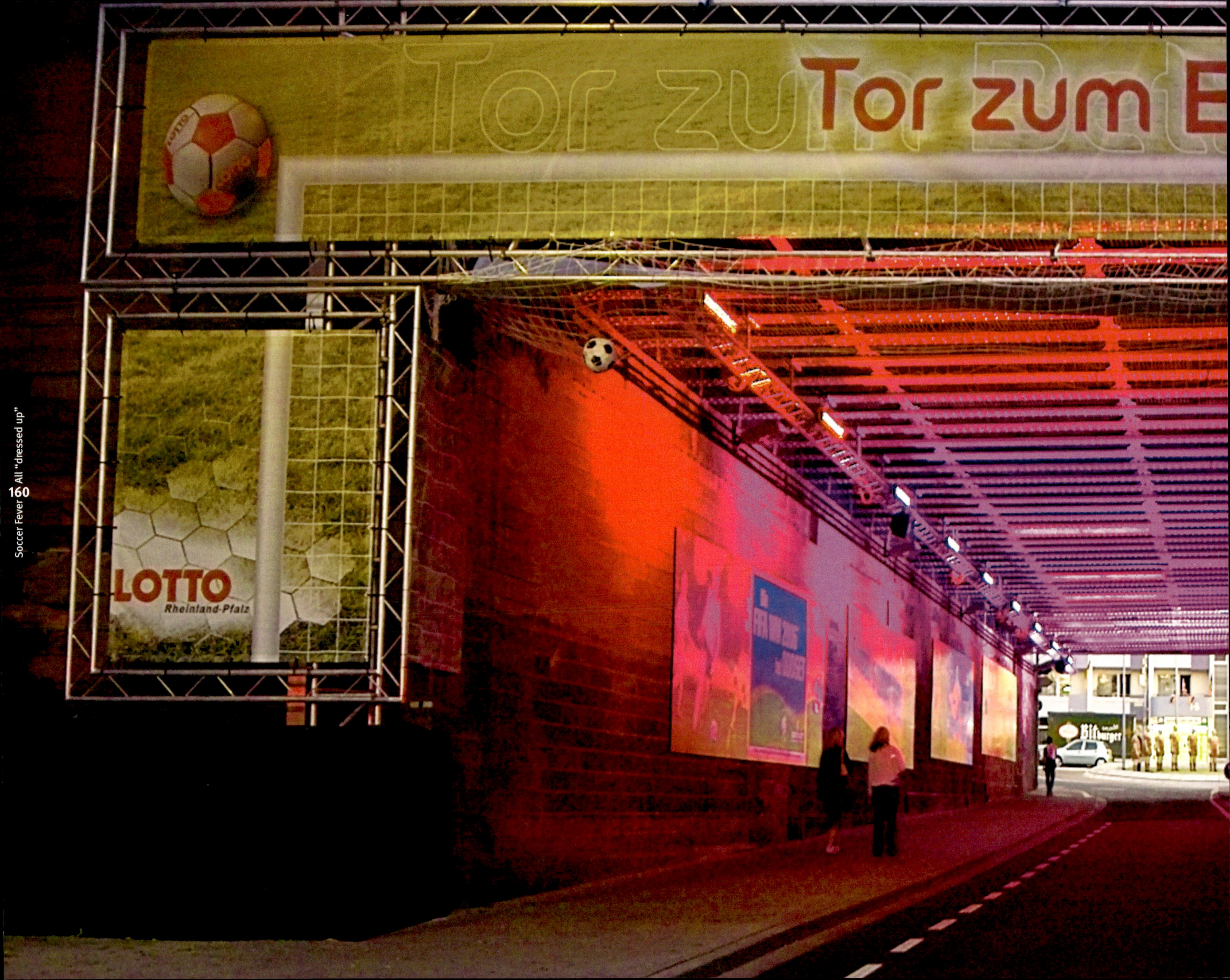
Tor zum
LOTTO
Rheinland-Pfalz

The sound and light installation in the underpass at the main train station, paired with historical soccer photos, was a small exhibit on its own. Talking about light: Numerous buildings in the city were illuminated, becoming brilliant centers of interest, from the police presidium to the finance office. At the city hall, the letters "WM" were blinking as though they were dancing to the Goleo tune. And even some manhole covers were "radiating" in diabolic red.

Zum Betzenberg

QUOTE ...

"THE WORLD CUP HAS changed the city – in the way it looks and in the minds of the people."

Bernhard J. Deubig,
Lord Mayor, Kaiserslautern

All "dressed up"

Of course, a vivid souvenir business was also going on. T-shirts, caps, shirts, mascots, and balls were the top favorites – and omnipresent in many stores. The World Cup Host City Kaiserslautern was also offering its own fan articles, such as commemorative coins and World Cup posters. Souvenirs and lasting memories.

SHOWING THE COLORS: Along the protocol route, about 300 flags in the World Cup design were flying.

All "dressed up"

The 2006 FIFA World Cup transformed Kaiserslautern into one large gallery. On huge posters, the pictures of successful players from Kaiserslautern were displayed on selected buildings in the city. Twelve scenes from Kaiserslautern's soccer history were shown on vinyl tarps of 80 to 800 square meters (860 to 8600 square feet) in size. The World Cup Gallery in Kaiserslautern thus probably became the world's largest open air gallery. In addition to the 1954 world champions, other Palatine soccer stars such as Hans-Peter Briegel, Andy Brehme, or Miroslav Klose were also immortalized in this action, which received major support from the Nationale DFB Kulturstiftung WM 2006 gGmbH foundation. For the so-called "blow-ups" developed by the Höhn Communication advertisement agency, a special style of illustration reminiscent of the pop art of Andy Warhol and Roy Lichtenstein was selected.

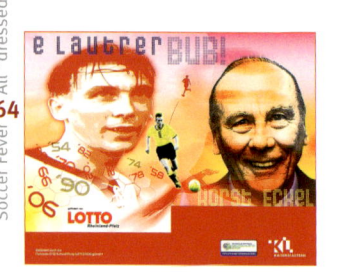

BY THE WAY: **The "recycling" of the giant posters also turned out to be extremely successful. The Westpfalz-Werkstätten (Western Palatinate Sheltered Workshops) produced World Cup souvenir bags in two different sizes from the material. These became an instant sales hit.**

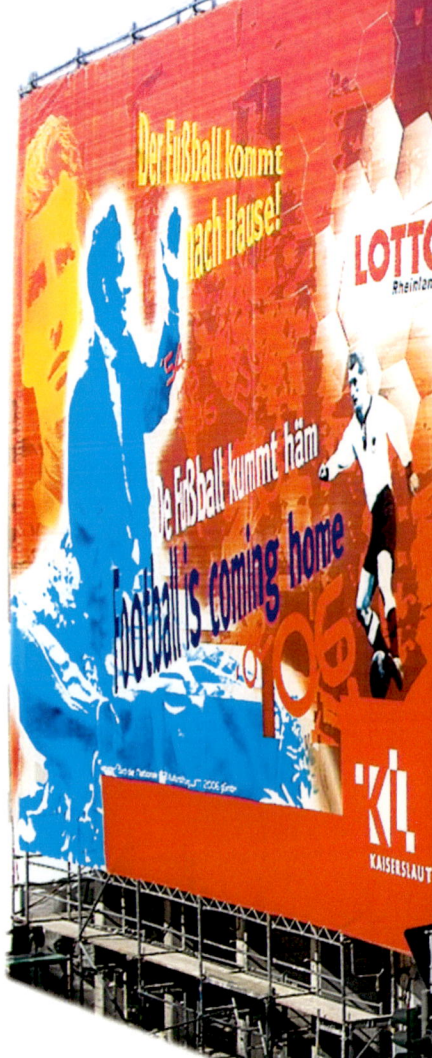

VOICES ...

" 'DE FUSSBALL kummt häm' (Football is coming home), this is what an advertisement campaign in the Palatinate is telling the interested visitor, and thus tranquil Kaiserslautern presents itself as the most beautiful, most cosmopolitan, and most Australian city in Germany on the third day of the round of sixteen."

11 friends, Germany

All "dressed up"

Much has already disappeared again from the cityscape. What definitely remains is a sign post showing the distances to the capitals of the teams hosted here. Signs that will certainly cause a little nostalgia every now and then.

10623 km Paraguay (Asunción)

nidad & Tobago (Port of Spain)

Australien (Canberra) 16505 km

Japan

Saudi-Arabien (Riad) 4346 km

USA

Spanien (Madrid)

Italien (Rom) 914 km

QUOTE …

"ALL GUESTS felt very well here, many want to come back. Is there any greater compliment for a host?!"

Erwin Saile,
World Cup Coordinator

VOICES ...

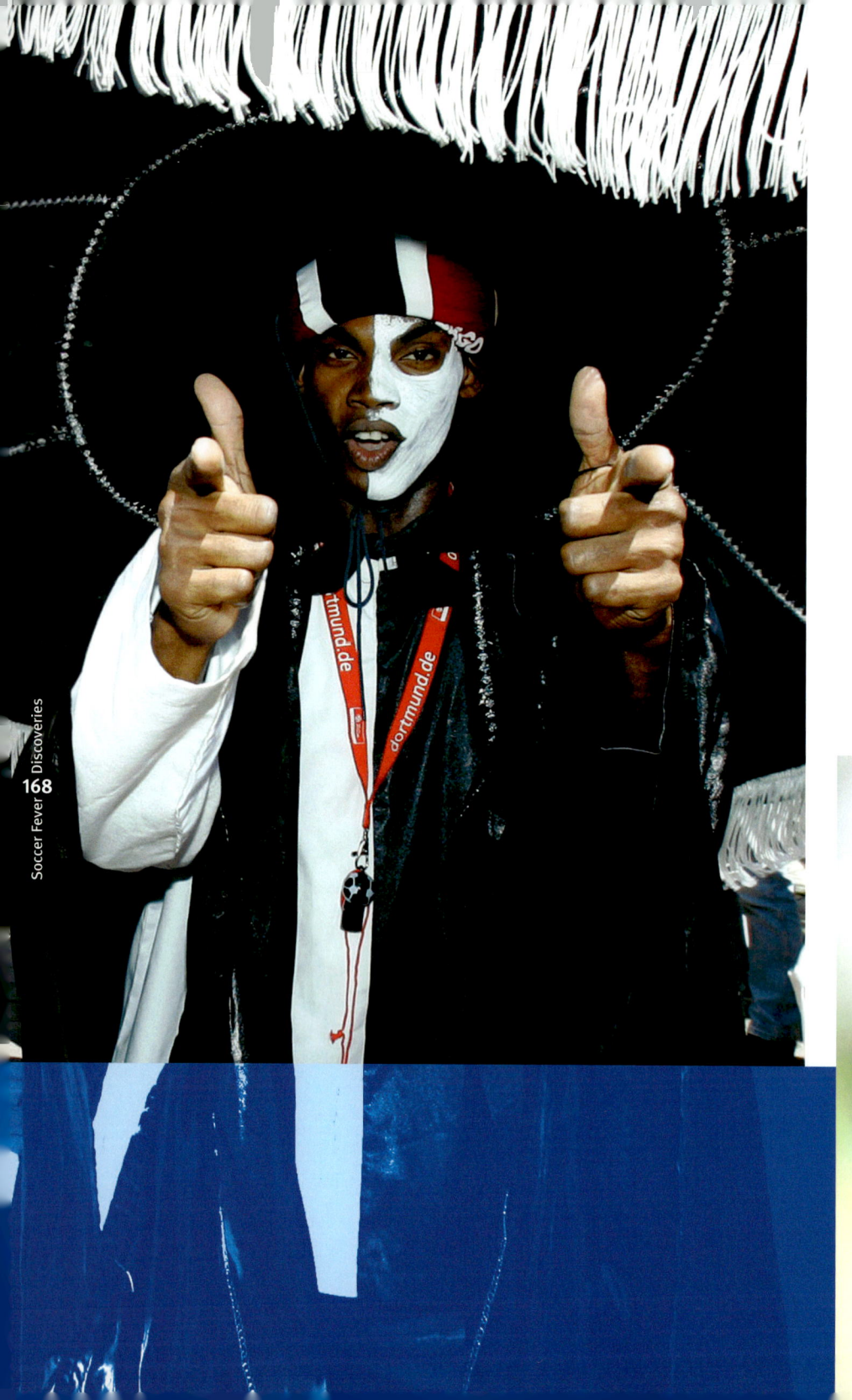

"THIS FLAG-WAVING GERMAN self-discovery has, in a sense, been the overriding outcome of this World Cup. Stereotypes about the country, such as its strong love for discipline and order, turned out to be the biggest error of a tournament held with a festive character and with the Germans' ebullient generosity."

New York Times, USA

Discoveries

MOMENTS ...

BECAUSE SOME Australian and English fans did not remember exactly anymore on which P+R parking lot they had parked their rental cars, two members of the World Cup Office called the city's driver service in order to search the parking lots Schweinsdell and Einsiedlerhof, which were the two possible choices, together with the fans. Since the driver on duty, a city volunteer, had filled in for someone else and did not know the area that well, the World Cup Office employees spontaneously got into the van, too, and guided the little group through the downtown area. By the way, all fans found their rental cars again.

...

Discoveries

The German fans discovered a lot of things during this World Cup. Odd things, amusing things, quaint things, and touching things. But they also discovered themselves. The observers from all over the world celebrated the "new Germans" in an almost exuberant manner. Apparently, we had not been known before as being so cosmopolitan, so friendly, and so relaxed.

But interaction was the key to making this mega-event so successful. We also discovered a lot. The World Cup was a crash course in hospitality. And we learned very quickly. Because our guests also made it very easy for us. They felt at home, but they behaved like noble visitors: eager to learn and without prejudice.

Many different cultures were guests in Kaiserslautern. Ethnology "live". The people were as different as the nations they represented. If you wanted to learn, you could learn a lot. The love for soccer (and for parties) unified them all. And opened up the chance to discover something new.

172

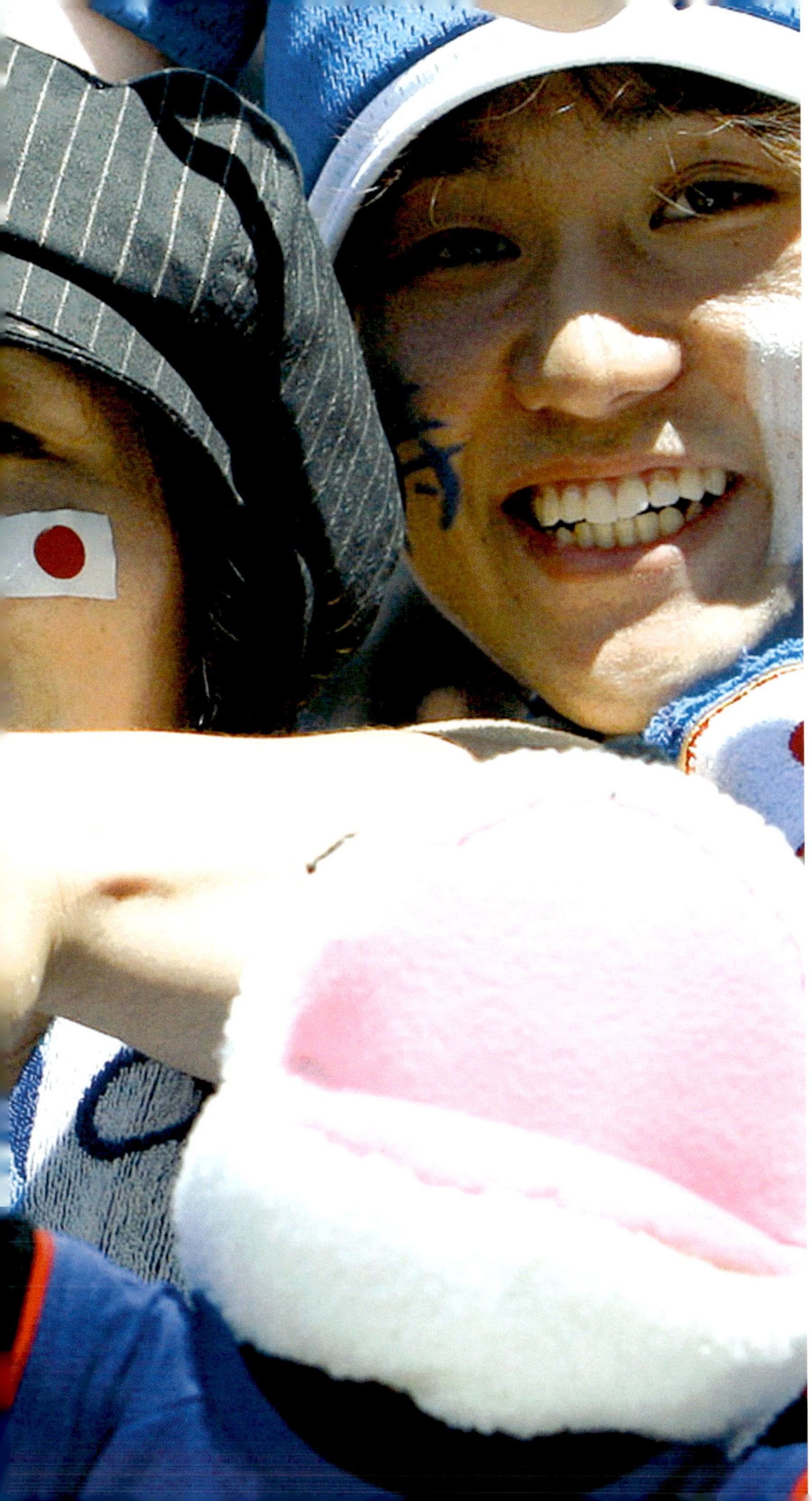

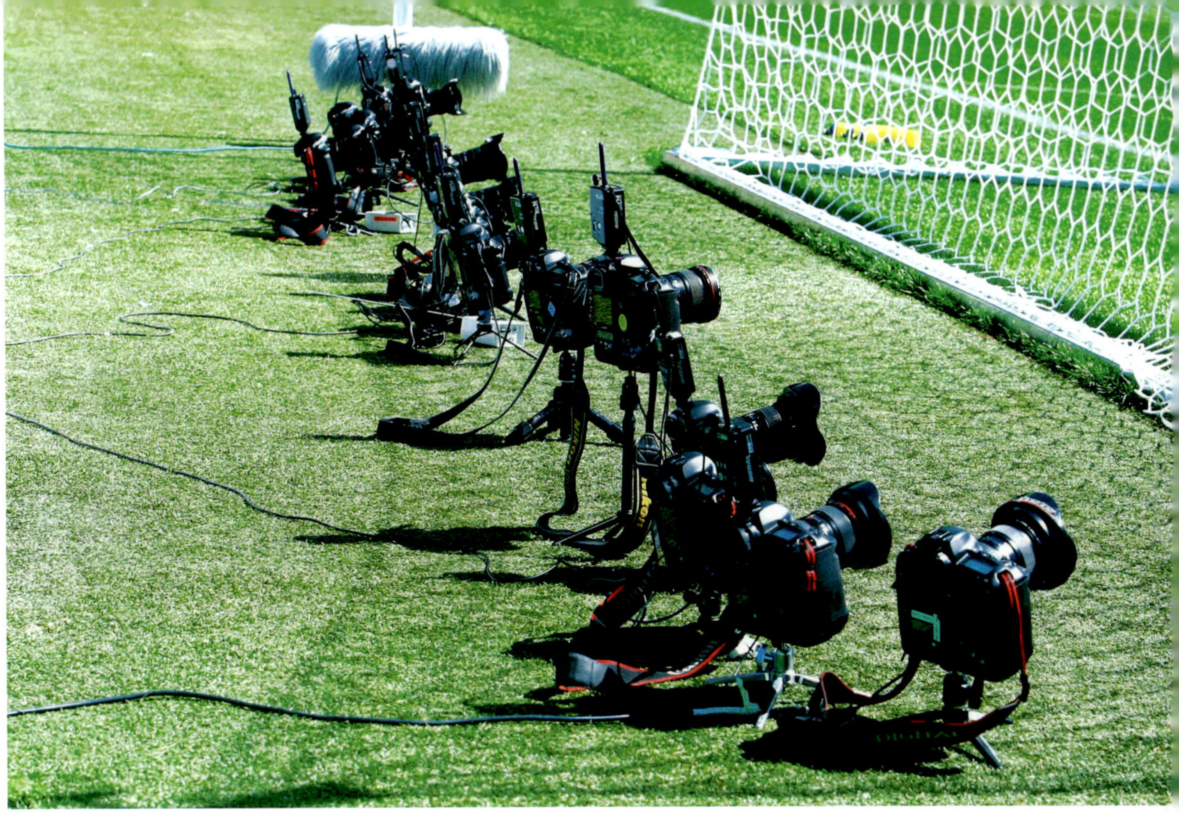

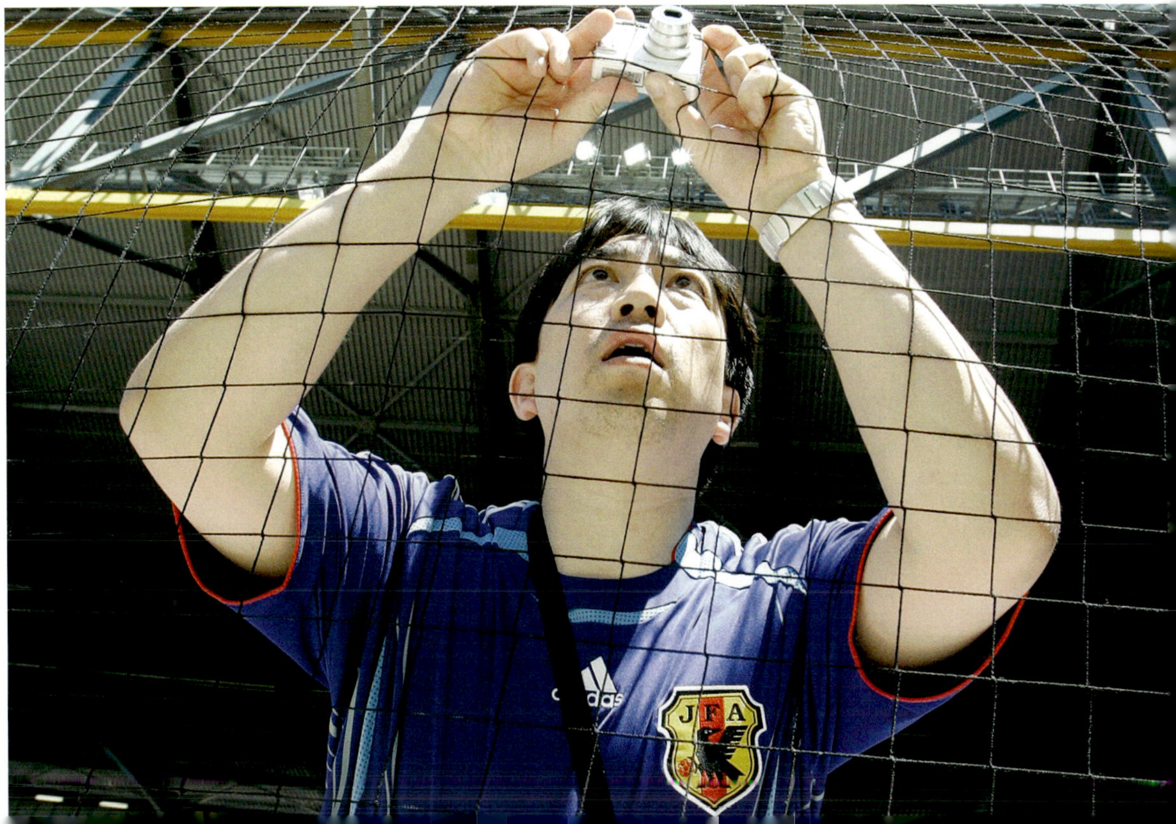
adidas
JFA

Discoveries

Kaiserslautern as a host city was also lucky, of course: The sun put on a wide smile and the German national team kept fueling the atmosphere in the whole country. There were no riots, no major accidents. This atmosphere was also internalized by the population, with long-term effects. In a survey performed by the University of Hohenheim, 95 percent of the residents of Kaiserslautern stated that the city is one of the winners of the World Cup. Top rated in Germany. In other areas, too, Kaiserslautern has achieved proud results. For instance, arrival and departure were studied by the University of Kaiserslautern – and were rated as having been extremely successful. Incidentally, this coincides with a study performed by the German automobile club ADAC, according to which the traffic flow in Kaiserslautern during the World Cup was the best among all host cities. In addition to that, we were also the cleanest World Cup host city. And we had the friendliest FIFA volunteers of the entire republic. This is not what we say, but rather renowned universities, including Johannes-Gutenberg-Universität in Mainz. They found out that 76 percent of the foreign guests would like to visit Kaiserslautern again some time. Welcome back! Eventually.

HUNTING FOR TICKETS: *The soccer fans thought of many ways of how to still get a ticket for some match or another.*

VOICES ...

"IT MAY BE that the black-red-gold costume ball got more and more disconnected from the actual event the more time passed. And a little absent-mindedly, the Germans in the end reinterpreted their little finals as having been the biggest match of the tournament. Jürgen Klinsmann was at once fitness coach and motivator for an entire nation. It may not matter so much what remains of this after the World Cup. To be able to influence the image of a country and its people is one of the phenomena that can emanate from great soccer tournaments."

Basler Zeitung, Switzerland

177

MOMENTS ...

KAISERSLAUTERN WAS the only World Cup host city to use motorcycle guides on the days of the matches in order to direct travel buses to their parking lots within the city limits as fast as possible. This service was met with great acceptance by the bus drivers and was initiated by the Motorradclub MIG from Kaiserslautern. This club mainly consists of city employees who had spontaneously agreed to take over the entire bus parking management.

Many hard-working helpers

The fact that the World Cup host city Kaiserslautern was rated as the cleanest city in a survey performed while the World Cup was still going on is clearly thanks to the more than 60 city sanitation workers. But in other areas as well, this World Cup could not have been mastered without the many volunteer helpers and official employees. The approximately 2,000 police officers employed each day filled the old-fashioned expression "The Police – your friend and helper" with new life, practically re-invented it.

Employees of the municipal public order office distributed plastic cups to ensure a "glass-free downtown area". All appeared to somehow have been infected by the good atmosphere.

DOC
DOC
DOC

ASB

Feuerwehr
112
Landkreis
Südwestpfalz
45
PS-8125

QUOTE ...

"THE ENTIRE REGION, its people, the city of Kaiserslautern, but especially soccer, are the clear winners ... All those who did the preparations performed excellent work with dedication and passion."

**Ottmar Walter,
1954 World Champion**

■ ■ ■

Soccer Fever | Many hard-working helpers

182

Many hard-working helpers

More than 400 city volunteers and about 1,000 volunteers from the FIFA OC assisted the organizers, lent a helping hand, informed guests, and were friendly ambassadors of this city. About 9,500 helpers from the fire department, medical services, German military, and the technical relief organization guaranteed on match days that in case of a catastrophe, help would be on site as fast as possible. Not everything that made this World Cup a success was a matter of coincidence.

MOMENTS ...

ALEXANDER AUER, 17-year-old student at Barbarossaschule, found an admission ticket for the match Italy against the USA before the match started. When he could not find the owner of the ticket near the place where he had found it in Malzstraße, the city volunteer turned the ticket in at the ticket center in Kohlenhofstraße – despite being offered 800 euros for the ticket. In appreciation of his honesty, Kaiserslautern World Cup Coordinator Erwin Saile presented him with a ticket for the match of the round of sixteen Australia against Italy.

Bereitstellungsraum Quartermaster →

A lot of this was due to the many employees who organized the World Cup because it was "their official duty": At FIFA, at the Organizing Committee, at the state, and at the city's World Cup Office. There, about 15 members of the World Cup Office under the leadership of World Cup Coordinator Erwin Saile worked for four years to create all the necessary conditions for this mega-event to go off smoothly. City design, infrastructure, tourism, events, security, press, or logistics: All threads came together in the city's World Cup Office.

The World Cup Office got assistance from the "Agency Team World Cup Marketing KL", which included the advertisement agencies ANTARES, Barth, and Höhn Communication.

VOICES...

"KAISERSLAUTERN IS – and was – provincial with pleasure. In the best sense of the word. This is the only way to explain why so many citizens took part, warmly welcomed the World Cup guests, and made them enthusiastic. The impression that Kaiserslautern conveyed will be permanent. Among people from all over the world."

Die Rheinpfalz, Germany

G-SHOCK
ADJUST
TIME MEMO
NOCH
361
TAGE BIS ZUM START
15:12:23
FUNKUHREN
CASIO
MODE
RECEIVE
FIFA FUSSBALL-WELTMEISTERSCHAFT
DEUTSCHLAND
2006
KAISERSLAUTERN
FIFA WM-STADT
GERMANY
2006
OFFICIAL LICENSED
TIMEPIECE
Offiziell lizenzierte Uhr der FIFA WM 2006™. Hergestellt unter der Lizenz von CASIO.

Data, Figures, Facts, and Results of the 2006 FIFA World Cup in KL

33 billion	TV spectators worldwide watched the 64 World Cup matches
2.5 billion	TV spectators watched the five World Cup matches in Kaiserslautern
3.3 million	spectators attended the 64 matches of the 2006 FIFA World Cup
1.0 million	visitors came to the World Cup Host City Kaiserslautern during the World Cup
250,000	visitors visited the World Cup Internet website of the city of Kaiserslautern
230,000	spectators watched the five World Cup matches at Fritz-Walter-Stadion
210,000	liters of beer were served during the World Cup at the Fan Fest locations and on the World Cup Mile
205,000	spectators experienced the World Cup in Kaiserslautern in the public viewing areas
200,000	paper flags were given away to citizens and guests by the Tourist Information Office
140,000	bratwursts (grilled sausages) were sold in Kaiserslautern during the World Cup
85,185	jobs were created by the World Cup overall
30,000	overnight stays were recorded by the hotels in Kaiserslautern during the World Cup
15,000	bottles of wine were served in the Wine Village during the World Cup
9,500	helpers from the fire department, medical service, German military, and the technical relief organization guaranteed the fastest possible help in case of a catastrophe on match days
6,500	calls were received by the joint call center of city and police
6,300	fans spent the night at the fan camp during the World Cup
3,000	accreditations were issued by the city for employees, service personnel, and security personnel
2,000	police officers were on duty each day during the World Cup in Kaiserslautern
714	media representatives were accredited in the city of Kaiserslautern, another 800 per match in the stadium
64	city sanitation workers ensured that squares and streets were clean every day
1	city did it all – Kaiserslautern

Words of
thanks and tribute

Words of thanks and tribute

The Organizing Committee of the 2006 FIFA World Cup has thanked the city of Kaiserslautern for hosting the FIFA World Cup matches in Kaiserslautern in a letter signed by Franz Beckenbauer, Horst R. Schmidt, Wolfgang Niersbach, and Dr. Theo Zwanziger.

Dear Lord Mayor, Mr. Deubig,
dear friends and fellow workers in Kaiserslautern,

Yesterday, the series of the five World Cup matches in Kaiserslautern came to an end with the match of the round of sixteen between Italy and Australia. We as the OC Presidium would like to take this opportunity to say a first, spontaneous, very cordial thank you for your great commitment during the 2006 FIFA World Cup. As the smallest host city, where even on the last day 100,000 visitors – as many guests as there are citizens – gathered once again, Kaiserslautern has made a tremendous achievement in our overall World Cup campaign.

With an overall joyful and peaceful soccer festival, Kaiserslautern has proved before the eyes of the world public to be a warm and perfect host.

Easy-going, relaxed, and full of ideas, the city, the region, and the citizens realized our World Cup slogan "A Time to Make Friends" in practice each day. With this, you made a great contribution to the wonderful atmosphere during this festival of world soccer, which would probably not have been possible to achieve without the great commitment of Kaiserslautern and the other eleven World Cup Host Cities.

As far as the sports part is concerned, the World Cup in Kaiserslautern is now over. However, the fantastic World Cup atmosphere will stay with you, too; if nothing else, via the Fan Fest, which will continue until 9 July.

We wish you that you will now be able to continue enjoying this unique event in our country in a relaxed manner. After the end of the World Cup, we will find an appropriate opportunity to again thank you, Lord Mayor, your city and its people as well as all responsible officials and helpers, and to jointly take stock.

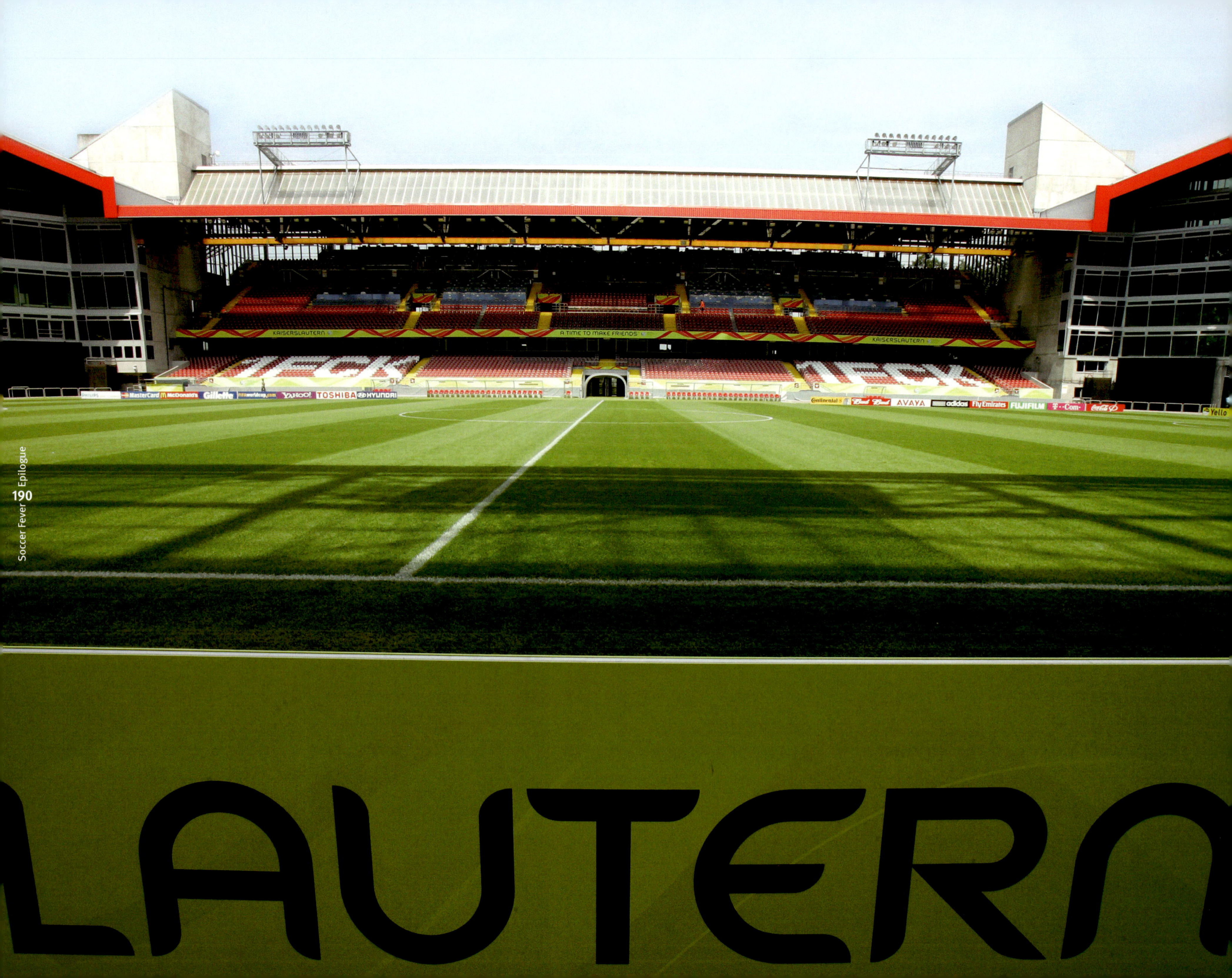
KAISERSLAUTERN
A TIME TO MAKE FRIENDS
KAISERSLAUTERN

Epilogue: World Cup Coordinator Erwin Saile

What remains of the World Cup?

For the finale, colorful lights once again "danced" over the city during the high altitude fireworks. Maybe the people of Kaiserslautern, the people of the Palatinate, will manage to carry over a part of this joy of life, of this serenity, into their daily lives. And some may have learned that a smile can open up another one's heart, and that a friendly word can work miracles. Let us therefore continue to live this "Summer Fairy Tale" together.

And what else will remain of the World Cup? In preparation for the 2006 FIFA World Cup in Kaiserslautern, about 150 million euros worth of investments were made into the stadium and into the infrastructure. Almost all of these measures will remain in place beyond the World Cup. The long-term effects should not be reduced only to parking lots and streets, however. Kaiserslautern and Rheinland-Pfalz have proven that they can handle the organization of such a mega-event.

Many institutions and offices collaborated on individual projects. This newly created network can generate positive effects well beyond the World Cup. In addition, the host of lessons learned can also be used for future mega-events. Organizational structures have been created that can be re-activated whenever the need arises. Plans for future events are already in the drawer.

The "radiating power" to the outside cannot be calculated in euros and cents yet at this time. Kaiserslautern was able to present itself to a global public. The increased popularity and the extremely positive image that was conveyed will have lasting effects and will – as we realistically hope – also entail economic success in the mid- and long-term. Particularly in the two continuously advertised core areas of IT site and tourism, positive effects will not be long in coming.

One should not underestimate the psychological effect of such a mega-event, either. The fact that the "province" mastered the top event World Cup results in a new level of self-confidence. The mentality of the people certainly has not changed radically, but maybe the people discovered new sides of themselves – and, in high spirits, showed these to guests from all over the world. The encounters with people from the most diverse countries and cultural areas were the real gain from the 2006 FIFA World Cup. And these do have a lasting effect. Permanently. Because they are strongly anchored in people's hearts.

Let's admit it: a soccer world cup is also "big business", a business where billions are at stake. The economic benefit of this event is hard to calculate for the World Cup Host City Kaiserslautern, but the advertisement and image value for the city alone is estimated by experts at about 200 million euros. There is no doubt that Kaiserslautern and the region will benefit from this mega-event for a long time to come. Financially and mentally.

I wish that all those who have experienced and lived this World Cup will keep this unique event in their hearts, and that they will continue to welcome the world as friends in the future, just like they did during the World Cup in our city.

May this book always remind you of the nice days in Kaiserslautern in the summer of 2006.

Erwin Saile
City of Kaiserslautern World Cup Coordinator

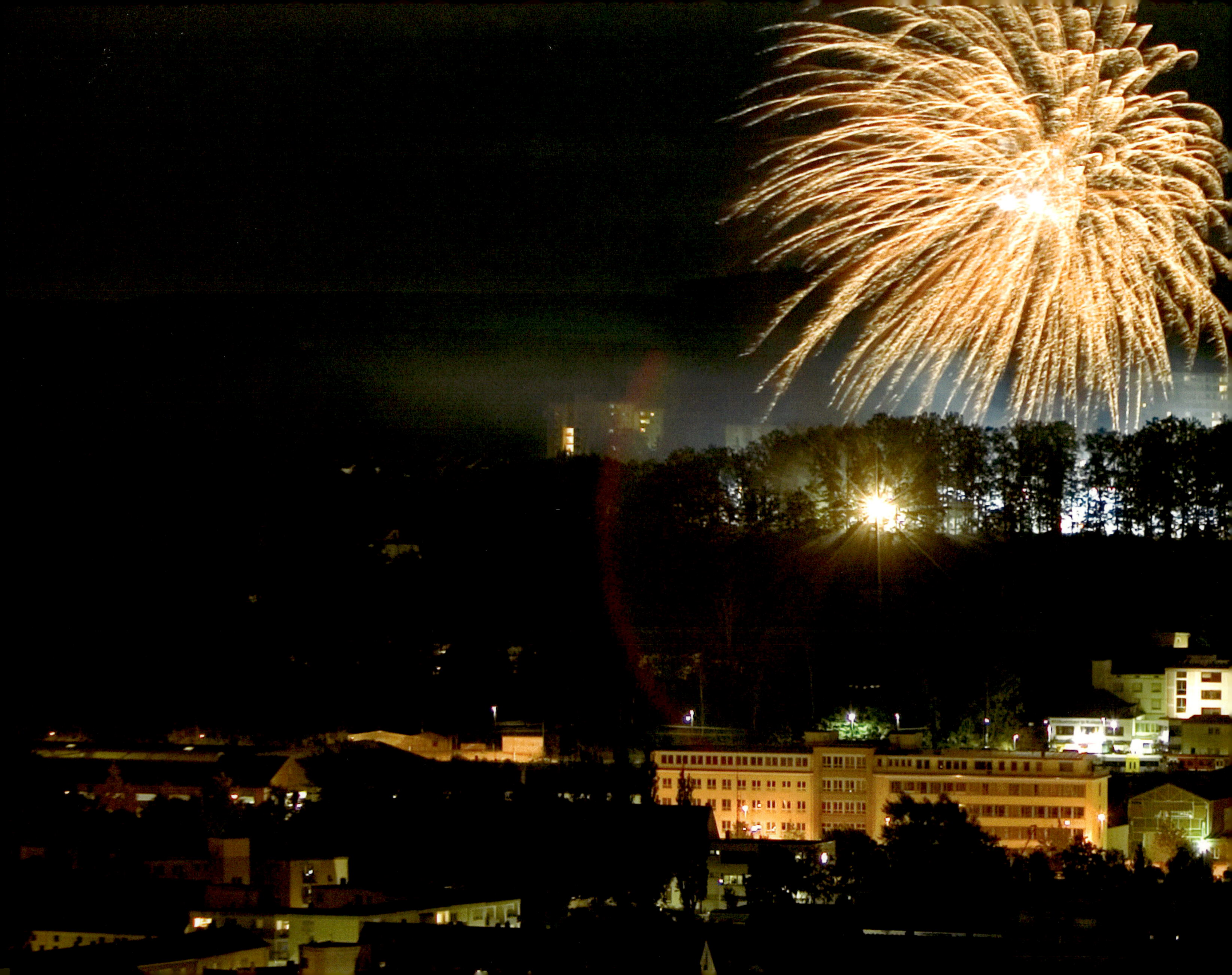

Soccer Fever –
31 Days
for Eternity